TO

EDITH MAUTNER FOYED

A TIME TO
REMEMBER

*From Austria to Bolivia,
Venezuela and the U.S.A.*

EDITH MAUTNER FOYER

Azalea Art Press

Berkeley, California

ISBN: 978-0-9849760-2-7

In memory of my parents,
David and Rosa Weingrün

ACKNOWLEDGEMENTS

Without the encouragement of my family, I would never have finished writing my story. I want to thank my younger son, Mark, who read and corrected my first draft and edited my final copy. A special thank you to Susan Mautner, my daughter-in-law, who not only encouraged me to write, but also helped select the photos from old family albums to include.

I would not have been able to finish the book without my eldest son, Willy, who helped me with my computer. I also want to mention Susan's sister, Karen Kronick, who urged me to finish my writing. Without her help, it would have taken me much longer to complete. I also appreciate the help and advice from my publisher, Karen Mireau, who helped to put my story together.

Edith Mautner Foyer

CONTENTS

INTRODUCTION

People always ask me, "How did you manage to escape from Austria?" I answer that I was fortunate to be able to leave Europe before World War II started. The next question usually is, "Why did you select Bolivia, and how was it living there at that altitude?" In truth, I did not select it, but I was glad that Bolivia accepted us.

We lived in La Paz, which is at such a high altitude that the climate and living conditions were very different from other cities in the world, even different from most other South American cities. That made it more difficult to explain my experience in just a few words. Later, my move to Venezuela was not what I expected, but somehow I overcame all the difficulties I encountered.

With the encouragement of my family, I decided to write my life story. It took me much longer than I anticipated, as it was much more work than I thought it would be to relate the details of how my life developed. I went from an innocent teenager in Europe, looking at the world through rose-colored glasses, to a grown woman in South America, able to confront all the challenges that presented themselves.

I have tried to tell about both the pleasant and difficult times I experienced realistically without making the events more dramatic.

When I think back on my life up until now, I must say it was really very unusual and I never expected it to be as it developed.

Edith Mautner Foyer

EARLY FAMILY HISTORY

Alter Weingrün was my paternal grandfather. My paternal grandmother's maiden name was Beckman. They had four sons, and the youngest was my father:

1. Adolph who married **Laura** and had three children:

Siegmund, who moved to South Africa.

Irenca was in Eritrea during the war. She later moved with her family to Montreal, Quebec.

Joseph had two children:

Steffa fled during the war with her husband and father to Rumania. Joseph was discovered by the Nazis and killed. Steffa and her husband survived and after the war moved to Australia. I visited her and her two daughters in Melbourne, Australia.

Fella remained in Krakow, Poland with her mother to take care of their properties. She and her mother did not survive WWII.

2. Ludwig was the father of two:

Genia survived the war in Theresienstadt concentration camp. After the war she came to Bolivia, but after a short while with my family moved to Brazil; I lost contact with her.

Ana, the second daughter, survived the years during the war in Siberia. She married and settled later in Haifa, Israel where she became a painter and had exhibits in Safed.

3. Frideck had one son **Edward** and both he and his son were sent to Mauthausen concentration camp, where they perished.

4. David, my father, was born April 1, 1884 in Krakow, Poland. He died in New York on December 1976. Around 1900, he went to Antwerp to learn the jewelry trade, and then moved to New York to join his brother Joseph, who was an agricultural engineer. Both brothers returned to Krakow, at the wish of their mother, who wanted her two sons back in Europe. My father moved to Vienna where he established himself as a jeweler.

I do not know much about my cousins on my father's side because they were mostly older, nearer my sister in age. Of all of them, I knew Edward, who was only two years older than I, and he came to visit us during the summer of 1937.

Selig Lustgarten married my maternal grandmother whose maiden name was Reich. My mother was also the youngest of four children:

1. Berta, whose married name was Zimmerspitz, was the mother of my cousins:

   Irene, who survived with Catholic papers in Warsaw. She later moved with her husband and daughter to Israel. I visited them there. Irene's daughter was married in Israel.

   Rella, and her husband also had Catholic papers, but they were discovered and denounced by a former employee and killed.

Mina Frydecki, had three sons, but only one, with his wife, survived.

2. Ignazy (Izek) lived in Warsaw, and had no children.

3. Zenek Lustgarten, youngest brother of my mother, was a lawyer before the war and spoke seven languages. He had two children younger than I. His whole family perished during the war.

4. Rosa, my mother, was born September 20, 1891 in a small village in the Tatra Mountains, now in southern Poland, close to the border of Austro-Hungary. She died in March of 1971 in New York.

FAMILY TIMELINE

Krakow, Poland
David Weingrün
b. April 1, 1884
(d. December, 1976 in New York)
m. Rosa Lustgarten
October 23, 1912
b. September 20, 1891
(d. March, 1971 in New York)

Vienna, Austria
David and Rosa Weingrün
1. Lilly Weingrün
b. March 25, 1914
(d. January, 2012 in New York)
2. Edith Weingrün
b. June 1, 1923

Hitler invades Austria
March 13, 1938
Kristallnacht
November 9-10, 1938

Bolivian visas received
December, 1938

Genoa, Italy
Departure for Bolivia
on the 'Virgilio', April 6, 1939

Ports of call:
Marseille, France
Las Palmas, Spain
La Guairá, Venezuela
Cristóbal, Panama Canal Zone
Guayaquil, Ecuador
Callao, Peru
Destination port: Arica, Chile
May 4, 1939

La Paz, Bolivia
June 15, 1940
Lilly Weingrün
m. Ernst Grab
1. Alfred "Freddie" Zenon Grab
b. October 14, 1946
(d. 1982 in New York)

Edith Weingrün
meets Karl Mautner, 1944

June 3, 1945
Edith Weingrün
m. Karl Mautner
(b. February 2, 1918 in Vienna, Austria)
1. Guillermo "Willy" Fred Mautner
b. February 20, 1948

Maracay, Venezuela
Move to Maracay
January, 1949

Caracas, Venezuela
Move to Caracas
December, 1949

Death of Karl Mautner
December 21, 1952

Edith Weingrün Mautner
meets Julius Foyer, 1955

Venezuelan citizenship
October 20, 1955

Departure for New York
on the 'Santa Maria'
August, 1956

New York
Arrival in New York
September, 1956

San Francisco, California
November 4, 1956
Edith Weingreen Mautner
m. Julius Foyer
(b. June 29, 1910 in Vienna, Austria)

San Mateo, California
American citizenship,
April 12, 1960

Julius and Edith Foyer
1. Mark Stephen Foyer
b. May 2, 1962

December 22, 1973
Willy Fred Mautner
m. Susan Springer
(b. September 16, 1949 in Palo Alto, California)
1. Carl Irving Mautner
b. December 10, 1982 in Seattle, Washington
2. Max Richard Mautner
b. August 2, 1987 in Orinda, California

Death of Julius Foyer
September 6, 1997

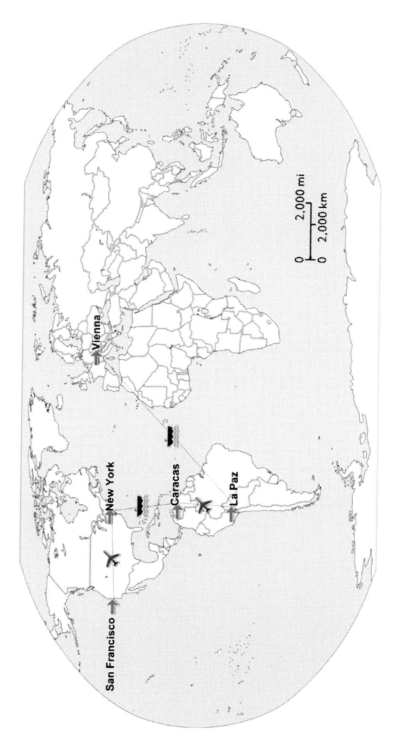

San Francisco

New York

Vienna

Caracas

La Paz

2,000 mi
2,000 km
0
0

EUROPE

FAMILY LIFE IN VIENNA

My parents David Weingrün and Rosa Lustgarten were wed in Krakow on October 23, 1912. They lived in Vienna where my sister Lilly was born on March 25, 1914. During the First World War, my father served in the Austro-Hungarian army as a weather observer for the air force. During the war, my mother took Lilly to Krakow, to stay with her family, and after the war they returned to Vienna.

David Weingrün and Rosa Lustgarten's engagement photo, Krakow, Poland

I was born in Vienna on June 1, 1923. During my childhood, we were comfortably middle class. In the summer months when I was a little girl, until age six or seven, my parents always rented a place close to Vienna to enjoy vacations away from the city. Usually it was not so far that my father couldn't join us for the weekends, and I believe he sometimes stayed longer.

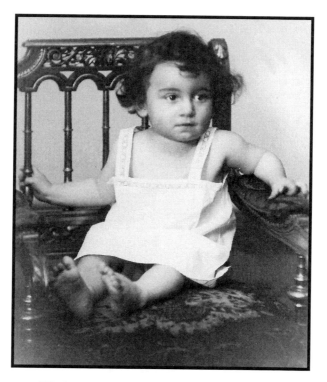

Edith at age one, Vienna, 1924

When the Great Depression began, it affected not only the United States, but also Europe. As a jeweler, my father's business suffered very much due to the world situation.

About the time I started school, our summer vacations changed, but I don't think I missed spending summers in those rented places. Instead, sometimes during the school vacation I went to summer camp. Twice I went to a camp program held at the summer residence of some Hungarian nobleman. It was very unusual in that it had a swimming pool, tennis court and bowling alley! But it was not what one might expect—the pool was definitely not heated and it was surrounded by trees. The leaves fell into the pool and made the bottom very slippery. We had to paint the lines on the tennis court ourselves, but still that is where I got my love of tennis. The bowling alley was very dusty affair, but we had great fun there. There was also a big yard with fruit trees and a vine-covered arbor, something new for me, growing up as I did in the city.

Edith and Lilly, 1930

When I was ten years old, I spent one summer in Krakow with my mother's family and met everyone. A few weeks were spent with my cousins on my mother's side in Myslenice. While in Myslenice my cousins showed me a house where either my grandparents or great-grandparents used to live. My father's family also lived in Krakow, but at that time I met only my grandfather. I must assume this was because all the others were away on summer vacation.

When I was twelve or thirteen years old, I joined the Jewish swim club, Hakoah. During the winter months I went swimming there in a heated indoor pool and for the summer there were outdoor facilities. The club was not too far from where we lived, and I had a summer season pass. I met my friends there and enjoyed it very much. I trained to compete in backstroke and was pretty good at it, but never set any records.

My father liked to hike very much and, weather permitting, we went most Sundays for a daylong walk. My mother prepared a picnic which we put in our backpacks and off we went. Sometimes we took the streetcar to the end of the line, which ended at the Vienna Woods, and other times we went by train, a little further. At noon we unpacked our lunch at some meadow where there was usually a little restaurant or beer garden, where you could get soups and refreshments. After a nice rest we continued to walk. My parents went to a coffeehouse every Saturday evening to read all the different newspapers.

On Sunday afternoons during the winter months, we usually went downtown for a walk, often ending up at a Viennese pastry shop (Konditorei), or other times we went to the Schönbrunn Palace where there was a beautiful conservatory with tropical plants, and then we would go afterwards to a Viennese coffee house which was close by. In later years my sister did not come with us anymore, especially during the winter when she liked to go skiing, as she had her own friends by then. Occasionally my father took me to a museum. There was a technology museum he liked very much, and then there was also the Kunsthistorisches Museum, a museum of art for paintings. There was a small painting in a corner, of a fish market. I don't know the artist, but I still remember the painting. I believe it was by a Flemish painter and was hung close by to the paintings of Bruegel.

My father was always very interested in new inventions. He himself was constantly working on innovations in the manufacture of jewelry. Twice a year, Vienna had an industrial exposition, which he always attended. My mother told me a cute story: It was during summer and my father came home from such an exhibit and told my mother, "There is a machine where you can hear music, even if it is played many blocks away." My mother answered, "Well, now it is summer and the windows are open, that's how you can hear it." That was the first time my mother heard about radio. Our first radio was a tiny little box with earphones and sometimes, if someone closed the door or walked into the room, you lost reception. Later, when I must have been about twelve years old, we got an amplifier with which we could hear broadcasting from Milan, Italy or some other places outside Vienna. Vienna had only one radio station then, which was run by the government.

GENOSSENSCHAFT DER JUWELIERE GOLD- UND SILBERSCHMIEDE

BENVENUTO CELLINI

Die
Genossenschaft der Juweliere,
Gold- und Silberschmiede
in Wien.

beurkundet hiermit, daß Herr
„David Eliasz Weingrün"
seit 23. April 1910
das Meisterrecht derselben besitzt
und die Einverleibungsgebühr, wie
umstehend ersichtlich, entrichtet hat.

Für die Genossenschaft:

Der Vorsteher-Stellvertreter Der Vorsteher.

David Weingrün
Master Jeweler Certificate

MY EDUCATION INTERRUPTED

In Vienna, four years of primary school and four years of secondary school were obligatory. After eight years of schooling, one either started to learn a trade, or one went on to higher education. As my sister went to a business school, it was assumed that I should go, too. Only I had different ideas. I said, "I don't want to write letters which somebody dictates to me, I want to be the one who dictates."

Because my sister was much older than I, she had her own group of friends, and in general they ignored me completely, with one exception—Otto Wallstein. I liked Otto because he always brought me candies. When he asked me where I would continue my studies I answered that I really was not sure. He had a small knitting factory and suggested that I could go to a school for the textile industry. Generally, it was difficult to be accepted, but he knew one of the professors. He had gone to school with him, and I could get a recommendation, which I actually did not need, because I had good grades in the secondary school.

I enjoyed the technical school very much and actually it was a very happy time for me, although it was very short. I started at the school in September 1937 and Hitler occupied Vienna in March 1938. I had big plans: I wanted to become an engineer in the textile industry, which at that time was very unusual for girls. I was not sure whether to specialize in mechanical engineering, involving calculation and estimating, or chemical engineering. Unfortunately, those dreams didn't come true.

In Austria, primary and secondary schools were gender segregated. In the textile school it was the first time that I was in a class with boys. I was one of only a few girls, as this was not a profession that interested many girls, even though the department I attended included knitting and design. In my class, about one-third of the students were girls, while the weaving and chemical departments had hardly any girls. The curriculum was very difficult and most classes started with fifty students; at graduation usually only half were left.

Austria was a Catholic country. Probably over ninety percent of the population was Catholic. In primary and secondary school you always knew who was Jewish, because at the beginning of each school day, we all had to stand and say a prayer. Jewish kids were excluded, which pointed right away to who was and wasn't Jewish. This is why I am very much against prayer in school. There were a few Protestant kids in my class. They prayed too, but there was no one of Islamic faith or any other. A priest came to teach the Catholic kids, and during those lessons, we had free time. We Jewish kids had religious instruction mostly in the afternoon.

Austria was always pretty anti-Semitic, but I didn't pay much attention to it. It was a way of life. While in secondary school, I belonged to the Jewish swim club. Some kids in my class belonged to a Christian club, I think the name was Evans and sometimes we had arguments, even some fistfights. My friend Erika Deutsch was very strong, and she could beat anyone, but all that changed on March 13, 1938.

In the middle of February 1938 I went on a ski trip for one week to the Austrian Alps with my textile school classmates. It was my only ski adventure ever. Only part of our class went and we were all girls. Two of the other girls were Jewish, and we three shared a room. During that time Hitler called the Austrian Chancellor, Schuschnigg, to a conference in Berchtesgaden, the seat of Hitler's Nazi Party. That was the first time I had some concern of what could come, but being young and very optimistic, while we talked about it in our room, we tried to ignore it.

At that meeting in Berchtesgaden, the destiny of Austria was decided. Hitler demanded that Austria should have "free" elections to determine if Austria would join Germany and become one country. The elections were called for March 13th. The weeks before the elections were pretty noisy. Everywhere there were banners pro and con, marches, etc. On Thursday March 9, in the evening, I went swimming as usual, and on my way back, a main street, which I had to cross to go home, was full of people. By the time I arrived home, my father was also out to see what was going on and when he returned he said, "Things don't look good." You have to understand, we did not have television and the radio station was government run and full of propaganda.

The next morning when we got up—I don't recall how we heard it—the elections were cancelled and German troops were entering Austria, "according to the wish of the people." The next thing I knew, the sky was full of airplanes. In 1938 when you saw an airplane you looked up, because it was very rare and suddenly I saw so many airplanes, that I could not

10

even count them.

This was the end of Austria as I knew it and it was a very big change for the entire world.

THE FAMILY IN VIENNA
OF THE "ANSCHLUSS"

My father saw right away that for Jews there was no future in Austria. Hitler's army entered Austria on Friday and on Monday my father went to the Australian Consulate to find out if he and his family could settle in Australia. Why my father had Australia in mind I don't know. My father had the good fortune to have artistic and technical skills in the design and making of fine jewelry, which enabled him to work anywhere without knowing the language of the country. He was truly an artist and his work was well recognized. I don't say that only because I am his daughter and taking pride in what he produced.

The information my father received at the Consulate was not very encouraging. He was told that to enter Australia you had to prove you had a certain amount of foreign money. I think that was to show that besides having a profession that could support yourself and your family, and that you didn't arrive penniless. It was called "Landungsgeld." Naturally, we did not have any foreign money. My father wrote to my uncle Joseph, who was living in Krakow, Poland, asking him if he could help us. His answer was that there were so many Jews living comfortably in Germany that surely the whole thing was only temporary. He reminded my father that he was not so young anymore, (he was at that time age 54) and too old to go and move around the world. Little did he know what was to come.

In July, my grandfather Alter Weingrün, who was about eighty-five, passed away. According to my Uncle Joseph he did not want to live anymore and somehow saw what was coming. Before his death, my uncle had to promise his father that he would help us to leave Austria, which as you will see he later did. Unfortunately, he himself never thought that one day it would be necessary for him to leave, and when Hitler's army marched into Poland he escaped with his daughter, Steffa, and her husband to Romania. Close to the end of the war he was discovered by the Nazis and was killed.

At that time my sister, Lilly, worked for a company that sold animal feed. They had offices and agencies in different parts of the world, in part to buy different raw materials that were then combined and then sold. The owners' names were Jacobi & Furth, or something similar, and they were originally from Romania. At that time their main office was in Vienna. Lilly found out that they had an agent in Buenos Aires, and we were informed that as my father had a profession as a jeweler we would be able to immigrate to Argentina. The agent in Buenos Aires tried to help us to get the necessary visas to enter the country. When my parents finally got through all the paperwork, Argentina changed the rules for immigration. With this new information our hope to go to Buenos Aires ended. By that time, it was the middle of July and more and more countries had closed their borders to Jewish refugees. Going to the United States was for us impossible. At that time to immigrate to the United States you needed a relative to sponsor you. We did not have any relatives in the States, and there was a law, which I believe lasted until the mid-1960s, that allowed only a certain specific number of people being born in certain countries to immigrate. For my parents who were born in what in 1939 was Poland, the quota was very low and already filled. Although my father had been in New York during the years 1909 or 1910, the documents of his stay were destroyed because it would have been dangerous for him when he joined the Austrian Army during WWI to have documents showing that he ever lived in the United States.

The situation itself in Vienna became more and more dangerous for Jews, as sometimes police, without any reason, picked up men from the street and sent them to Dachau or Buchenwald concentration camps. Some were released after a certain time and for others only the notice that they had died came back to their families. Sometimes professionals, mainly physicians or other prominent people, were arrested. Two of my father's cousins, Dr. Max and Dr. Fritz Beckman, whom I called uncles, were lucky enough to survive Dachau. Later, when I came to New York, I saw them again.

During this time I learned a lot of geography. Growing up in Central Europe, I knew only of the so-called three "A.B.C." countries of South America—Argentina, Brazil and Chile. My geography teacher told us those were the only ones we needed to know anything about, as we would never visit any of those countries, nor were they very likely to come up in any conversation. My knowledge of Asia was also very limited. It turned out that during the summer of 1938, I met my old teacher on the street—she was a very religious Catholic and against Hitler and what he preached. She admitted how wrong she had been when teaching us geography and wished me good luck in finding a place to live and encouraged me to continue my education.

During that time my sister's boyfriend was Ernst Grab. They were to marry later and he became my brother-in-law. Both Lilly and Ernst worked in offices and worried that they would have to leave Vienna for an uncertain future, where their hope for an office job was very slim. Each started to take courses that might enable them to support themselves with work that didn't require knowing the language of some unknown country. My sister went to a cooking school and Ernst learned to make liquor and took a course for baking. As a matter of fact, Ernst enjoyed baking and in later years, even when living in New York, he was the baker for the family. By the middle of summer I believe both had lost their jobs.

Ernst had a brother, Kurt, who had just graduated from medical school a few months before Hitler invaded Austria. He had a classmate in medical school who was from Bolivia. Coming from Bolivia, and being a foreign student, he was pretty short financially. While the two friends studied medicine together, Ernst's mother invited the young man from Bolivia to stay for dinner, which he appreciated. He started to work at the Bolivian Consulate after Hitler came to Austria and there he was able to procure entrance visas to Bolivia for the two Grab brothers and for their sister Stella. Studying the encyclopedia, which was the only source we could go to for some information about Bolivia, we could not find out very much. Having no other choice, the two brothers got passage on a ship. Since Bolivia bordered Argentina, they thought if life in Bolivia was too primitive, they could always try to get to Buenos Aires. It was at that time we were also hoping to get to Argentina, so my sister and Ernst were hoping to meet there.

Ernst and Kurt left Vienna in the middle of September 1938, just as Hitler occupied the Sudetenland in Czechoslovakia. In the first letter Ernst sent home, he wrote: "La Paz is a nice city with nice buildings and a big boulevard, where on Sunday morning music was playing and people were well dressed and strolling around."

By the end of summer, any last hope to immigrate to Argentina was gone. Lilly's boss had moved the office to London and let Lilly know that for the moment he was unable to get her a visa to work in his office. However, he could get her a visa as household help and might be later to be able to arrange for her to work there. Having no other way to get out of Austria, Lilly agreed to it and left for London in the beginning of November 1938.

At that time we heard that a committee had been organized in England that offered the possibility for children to be sent to England for safety. My parents were able to register me for this, and I had a tentative date of January 1939 to leave Vienna. Lilly's boss also offered to help me if I could get to London, but the committee made all of the arrangements for finding sponsors for the children. This came to be known as the Kindertransport.[1]

---

[1] Kindertransport was composed of many individuals and organizations from all faiths that came together to rescue children from the atrocities occurring under Hitler. From

Once I was at a reunion of those children, now adults, and they talked about how some had a very difficult time in England. Not only did most never see their parents again, but also since they were very young, they felt lost and were not always treated well. As I recall, I was not afraid to leave my parents and go alone to England, as my sister was already there. I was very optimistic that my parents would follow me. On the other hand, I wanted to finish my education. At that time, many families could not leave Vienna together and were forced to split up, hoping they would somehow again be reunited. Some people were thinking that the whole thing was only temporary and that life would soon return to normal. My best friend, Erika Deutsch, went with the Youth Aliyah[2] to Israel. I don't know what happened to her parents or her brother.

My uncle Joseph was always very interested in the history of our family and prior to 1938 he found out that the chief rabbi of Dublin was named Weingreen[3]. He contacted the rabbi and was informed that we were somehow related. When it seemed that I might go to England, my mother wrote to him, asking

November, 1938—September, 1939 approximately 10,000 babies and children under the age of 17, mostly Jewish, were transported by ship without their parents to England. Most of these children never saw their parents again.

[2] The Youth Aliyah was founded to rescue Jewish children from the Nazis. Approximately 5,000 teenagers from all over Europe were relocated to Palestine before the outbreak of WWII and another 15,000 children, mostly Holocaust survivors were brought there after the war.

[3] Anglicized spelling of the family name Weingrün, also adopted by David and Rosa upon immigration to the U.S.

that in the event there was no other place I could stay, if he would be willing to take care of me and he answered in the positive. A few years ago, I was in Dublin and found a Weingreen in the telephone book. I tried to call, but nobody answered. It was during summer and he was probably on vacation. It would have been very interesting to meet him or his son.

By the time Lilly left for England, my parents were pretty desperate to get a visa somewhere in the world as one country after another closed its borders. The only way you could go somewhere legitimate was by getting a passage on a ship going to Shanghai. You could try to enter a country illegally, but most countries sent you back. A few succeeded in going to Switzerland. Later, my future husband Julius told me that he tried to cross the border to Switzerland, but was returned by the border police. I think that was one of the reasons he never wanted to go there as a tourist. Some lucky people succeeded in going to Belgium, but later Germany occupied Belgium and they were not so lucky anymore.

The situation in Vienna itself was quite bad for Jews. For instance, if my father went out and did not return at the expected time, we were always afraid that he was picked up on the street and sent to Dachau, the concentration camp. I think at the beginning of September my father's cousins, whom I mentioned earlier, Dr. Max and Dr. Fritz Beckman, returned from Dachau and had to leave the country within a certain time. But having no visa, the only way to leave Vienna was to go somewhere illegally. They succeeded in going to Belgium by crossing the border. Later somehow they managed to get to England. I believe their wives were able to get work in England as housemaids and the husbands could later follow them before the war started. After the war they moved to New York, where they practiced medicine again. In 1956, when I moved to the United States, one uncle guaranteed for me that I would not become a burden of the United States Government and I was allowed to immigrate.

Most people, at least officially, praised Hitler and what he stood for. There were some people who were not so happy with the situation, but were afraid to say anything. My good friend Trude Franzl lived in the same building as we did. Her apartment was one floor below ours. We were the same age and we spent a lot of time together. I was usually in their apartment or she was in ours, especially when we were in elementary school. Later we developed different interests. Her father was ballet master with the Vienna State Opera and at a very early age she started to take ballet lessons at the ballet school of the Vienna State Opera. One day, after Hitler occupied Austria, I met her on the stairwell and she told me, "Edith don't feel bad when I see you on the street and I do not greet you, as my father is a state employee and seeing us together might cost him his job."

As I always had spent Christmas night at Trude's home, this year, 1938, her parents sent their maid home and called me to be with them. They told me that if I were not with them, something would be missing. They even sent cookies to my parents, something they had never done before. Sometime later, I found out that Trude married an American officer in Vienna and was living in the United States. While corresponding with her, she wrote me that her daughter lived in Portland, Oregon. I suggested that if she ever visited her daughter I would come and visit her, even if it was just for one day. Her daughter thought that I should spend some time with them while Trude was in Portland. Although we had not seen each other for sixty years and during that time we had very different lives and experiences, the moment we met, it was if as we had said goodbye just yesterday. It was amazing how a friendship from childhood had never faded. I had a wonderful time in Portland but her home is now in Helena, Montana, where it is too difficult for us to visit each other.

KRISTALLNACHT—
NIGHT OF BROKEN GLASS

Days before November 10, 1938, rumors were going around that a young Jewish fellow attacked an employee at the German Embassy in Paris. We did not know if it was true, as the only news we could receive was controlled by the government. Somehow we had the feeling that this propaganda would be used against the Jewish population, but no one expected anything like the planned assault of Kristallnacht[4] with the terrible destruction life and property.

The day before, I had a very bad head cold and my mother suggested I should stay in bed to get over it. About seven o'clock in the morning, I heard some steps in the apartment above ours and a few minutes later our apartment bell was ringing. In front of our door were some S.S. men with our concierge[5]. They told my father to get ready to leave, but did not tell us where he was going to go and what was going to happen to him. We expected the worst.

The area in Vienna where we lived was not typically Jewish. In our apartment building were just a few Jewish families. Among them was the Sterk family. Their daughter Traude was my age and often played

---

[4] On November 9-10, 1938, over 7000 Jewish shops were destroyed and 1000 synagogues burned down by Nazi S.A. (Sturmabteilung) storm troopers. An estimated 91 Jews were killed and another 30,000 incarcerated in concentration camps.
[5] We later found out that our concierge was a big Nazi sympathizer.

with me. During the morning I telephoned Traude and she told me that her father was also taken away. They lived in a different part of the building and her mother asked us to come to visit them in the afternoon in their apartment. Due to the shock of my father being taken away, my cold was gone. My mother and I spent the afternoon with Traude and her mother trying to find out what was going on and hoping that our fathers would be home soon, but we were very pessimistic.

For dinner we returned to our home, not knowing where my father was or what happened to him. When we were getting ready to go to bed, our doorbell rang. In front were some S.A. men (Nazi storm troopers) with our trusted concierge, telling us that "for our own security" we would have to leave the apartment. They did not tell us where it would be secure for us to go at night and I was convinced that leaving the house at night and being in the street would not have been very safe either. They told us we could pack a little suitcase with the most necessary things and within a few minutes we would have to leave. They said they were going to seal the apartment. We had about ten minutes to grab the most important things, or at least those we thought we would need immediately. When we left the apartment, we did not know if we would ever be able to return.

We left the apartment with a very small suitcase, and we really did not know where to go. We had an aunt, actually a cousin of my father, who lived in another part of Vienna. Her husband was detained in the concentration camp Dachau, but we did not know what happened to her and her son. It was simply too dangerous to be on the street. When we left our

22

apartment, we saw light in the apartment of the Sterk family, and according to our doorman, they were still in their apartment, so we went to them. Their apartment was a very big apartment with two bathrooms, which was very unusual in Vienna. A few months before they were forced to take in another couple (they did not know the people before) who had to vacate their own apartment, because some official wanted it. The lady was very sick with cancer and at that time they still respected illness. We went to their apartment and were able to stay there. Traude moved into the bedroom of her mother and my mother and I stayed in Traude's room. There we stayed for nine days until my father was released.

Those were nine horrible days, as we did not know what happened to our fathers. Rumors were flying around that all the men were sent to a concentration camp. Traude and I decided we did not want our mothers to worry about what was going on and which rumors were true and which were not. We both were fifteen years old and we took on the responsibility for taking care of our mothers and seeing what we could do to get our fathers out. The next day we decided to go to the Jüdische Kultusgemeinde (the official office for Jewish affairs). It was located next to the Seidenstetten Temple, the synagogue I used to attend, and close to where we lived. When we arrived there we found the temple in shambles. I will never forget the sight of it—it used to be very beautiful. There at the Kultusgemeinde office we found out that some of the people who were removed from their homes were taken to a high school. We went there, but could not even get close to the city block where the school was located.

When we returned home, we did not give our mothers many details, partly because we did not know much and partly because we did not want to worry our mothers more. The only thing I let my mother do was to go to the police and see if we could get back into our apartment. The only information my mother got was that, "for our own security the apartment has to remain sealed until my father returned." On the other hand we did not know when my father would return. Usually when people were sent to the concentration camps they remained for many months or never returned at all. This was a very serious situation for us. As friendly and hospitable Traude's mother was, we could not camp in their apartment for a long period of time. The Sterks had a maid at that time, so we did not have to worry about cooking, etc.

After a few days, Traude had a postcard from her father and when we looked into our mailbox, we found a card from my father too, in which he wrote asking if his visa to go to England had already arrived. Traude's father wrote that her mother should get them passage to Shanghai.

When my father returned he told us that people were asked if they had a visa. Later we found out those without a visa or plans to leave the country were separated and sent to Dachau. My father who usually took things in stride realized that if he said he had a visa he might get out, which is what really happened. Mr. Sterk did the same. When we received the postcards, we at least knew that our fathers were alive and according to rumors, people who sent cards were not sent away, but that was only an assumption.

After nine days our fathers came home. My mother went to the police and as they had promised we were able to return to our apartment. In Vienna we did not have a refrigerator and the food in the kitchen was all mildewed and smelled bad, but we were happy to be home again and to have my father back, with his head shaved and a nine-day-old beard.

PROBLEMS IN LEAVING VIENNA

We were very happy to have my father home, but now we had another very big problem. When my father was released from the police, or S.S., he had to sign two documents. One was that he should never mention what he saw or what happened to him during those nine days he was detained. My father never spoke about it, even later when we were in Bolivia or in New York. The second document stipulated that he had to leave Germany within ninety days or be taken to a concentration camp. This was a very serious matter; after all, while he was detained he said that he expected to get a visa to England.

As my father had no visa to go anywhere, the threat was very frightening. By that time Ernst, my future brother-in-law, was already in Bolivia. We heard from Ernst's mother that if we sent him a cable and money to return a cable, he would able to send us a visa to Bolivia. After one week, we received notice that we had permission to enter Bolivia. The next problem was to get space on a ship to take us there. There were only a limited number of ships to the west coast of South America and the demand was very great. As there was also a visa for me, my mother decided if we were able get shipping space for me that I should come with them, so that we could be together as a family. This would also give another child the opportunity to leave Vienna with the Kindertransport.

Thankfully, we all got space on a ship. Ernst's parents, who received their visa at the same time, were able to get a space on the same ship, so we could all travel together. Lilly, by that time, also had a visa and planned to meet us in Bolivia. However, since she departed from England, she left on a different ship one month earlier than us. The name of our ship was the "Virgilio." It left Genoa at the beginning of April in 1939 and my father was able to extend his stay in Vienna until the middle of March. To validate our visa we had to show that we had the equivalent of thirty-six English pounds per adult person (at that time it was a lot of money). My uncle from Krakow deposited the money at the consulate in Genoa as proof and then during December we finally we had our visas to enter Bolivia.

While we were trying desperately to get a visa and later also a place on a ship to take us to Bolivia, we were informed that a neighbor who had a smaller apartment in our building had made a request that we leave the apartment, because he wanted to occupy it. Those requests were generally granted. We, as Jews, had no right to defend ourselves and we would be required to leave the apartment on the date he wanted to take possession of it. When he found out that we were leaving Vienna during March he behaved graciously and said that he could wait until we departed.

Now we had another problem, as the earliest available date for a place on a ship was April 6, 1939— the date the ship was leaving from Genoa—and my father had to leave Vienna by March 15. That meant that we had to stay for three weeks in Genoa. Being able to leave Vienna with only ten German marks, how and where could we live for those three weeks without any money? Here again Lilly's old boss was very helpful and I will be always thankful to him and his company. At that time there was a law in Italy that any profits you had made in the country, even if you were a foreign company, were not allowed to be taken out of the country. When my sister told her former boss about our problem, he said we should not worry, he would take care of us the minute we arrived in Genoa, and he was good to his word in the most wonderful way. He gave us the private address of the manager of his office and we were told that they would take care of us.

After we had our visas, it was time to liquidate our apartment, which meant to sell everything, with the exception of what we planned and were able to take with us. For my father it was very important to take the tools of his trade along, so that he would be able to work as a jeweler. To be allowed to take any tools or valuables with you, one needed special permission. This was done just to make it more difficult to be able to establish again in some other place and lead a normal life later. My father applied for it and got the permission for the tools, but no other kinds of valuables like silver or jewels. While we had a dispatcher packing our things, two S.S. men were watching what went into the crates, to be sure that we did not include some things for which we did not have a special permit. Besides the tools we were only allowed to pack household things, like dishes, linen and personal clothing.

It was kind of sad seeing the things I lived with all my life left behind in the apartment, but in my optimism, I was already looking forward to a new life in Bolivia where I would be able to walk on the street without any fear of harassment. Being a very young teen, it was some kind of adventure, and I was also very glad that I would not be separated from my parents and my sister.

Finally our departure time neared. The apartment was quite empty. The crates were packed and supposed to be shipped to Bolivia as soon as possible. It looked as if everything was in order. On March 15th Hitler occupied Czechoslovakia and we were afraid the Germans might close the borders, but in this respect nothing happened.

I don't know what happened with our concierge; he wanted to give us some trouble in leaving the house, so my parents had to take our hand luggage to the train station the night before our departure, so that he was not aware when we were leaving. We left the house the next morning without any luggage and went by streetcar to the railway station. My mother felt pretty bad to secretively leave a place she had lived happily for many years.

Because of Germany's occupation of Czechoslovakia, all the houses had Nazi flags to celebrate the event. When, from the train, we saw the first house without any flags, we knew we were out and saved. On the train were other Jewish travelers. We all started to smile and embrace each other. Happy to escape, although not knowing what life was awaiting us, we were all sure that everything would work out fine.

Passport Photo, Edith Weingrün, 1939

Passport Photo, Lilly Weingrün, 1939

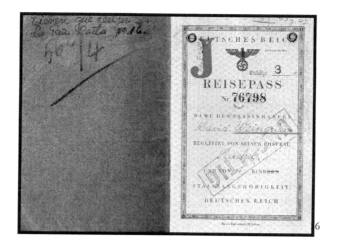

Passport for David, Rachel
and Edith Weingrün
January 16, 1939

---

[6] Our passports were marked with a "J" for Juden or Jewish. In keeping with Nazi regulations, my Mother's name was listed as Ruchel instead of Rosa to further identify her as a Jew.

BOLIVIA

FREE AT LAST,
CROSSING THE OCEAN

Upon arrival in Genoa, we went to a hotel to clean up and to leave our hand luggage. As we were instructed to do, we took public transportation to the home of the manager of the office. The wife of the manager was expecting us and informed us that she had made a reservation in a boarding house, which was very close to her own home. Actually we could see from her window the place where we would spend the next three weeks. It was in a lovely residential area, the sun was shining and from my room I could see the ocean for the first time in my life. As Austria is an inland country, I had never seen such a sight before. We never met the manager personally. It was his wife who had arranged everything for us and it could not have been better. She also gave us some spending money, because she knew coming from Austria we did not have any money. After all the stress we had experienced during the last year, their help allowed us to really enjoy those three weeks.

The boarding house served three meals each day. We very much enjoyed the Italian food and all the different kinds of pasta and also different kinds of dishes we were not used to. Although when we left Vienna there was no food shortage, fruits like oranges, lemons, bananas (I mean imported fruit), were in short supply. Other food, though not rationed, sometimes was not available.

We were in Genoa on Palm Sunday. It was a beautiful sunny day and we took some public transportation to the suburb of Nervi. There I saw lemon trees for the first time; they reminded me of a quote from an old German classic by the author Goethe, "Let's go to the country where the lemons bloom." All the church bells were ringing and it felt like paradise to me. It was also the first time I saw palm trees outside. The only ones I had ever seen in Austria were in the conservatory in Vienna at the former summer residence of the King of Austria who reigned before World War I. During our stay in Genoa, the parents of Ernst and a cousin, Walter Breslauer, joined us in the boarding house. We were kind of a family in a foreign land.

In Vienna, my father made jewelry for export and was very pleased to find some of his work in the finest jewelry stores of Genoa. However, my father was not to do this kind of work in Bolivia, as there was neither the market for this kind of luxury nor availability of the raw materials like cut diamonds. Later, he could get semi-precious stones from Brazil. It was not until he moved to New York that he could resume doing work similar to what he did in Vienna. Shortly after we arrived in La Paz, the war broke out and people had other interests.

While we were in Genoa, my father visited the Bolivian Consulate where my uncle had deposited our "Landungsgeld" with the intention that we would receive it. It was our money. The Consul explained to my father that he could not hand over the money, because we might spend it before arriving in Bolivia and then have no money when we arrived there. Or it might be that we would not go to Bolivia at all. But he assured my father that upon our arrival in La Paz the money would be there, deposited in the National Bank of Bolivia. It made some sense to us, although we would have preferred to have the money right away.

While we were in Genoa, my parents met an old acquaintance. He was recently released from the concentration camp in Buchenwald and was on his way to Shanghai. He was very happy to meet somebody with whom he could talk about old times. As his ship left a few days before ours, we went to see him off and wish him good luck for the future. The ship's name was the "Conte Biancamano." It was not a very happy atmosphere at the departure, as going to Shanghai was actually the last resort. You had to leave Germany and go to a place where you were accepted. At that time there was a very popular song: "A ship goes to Shanghai and never comes back…" When the ship left the dock the ship's orchestra was playing this song and everybody on the dock started to cry, as well as the passengers. Little did we know what would later happen to those who had visas to some European country. At the time, we thought they were the lucky ones.

I felt very fortunate to be going to Bolivia knowing there was a nice city awaiting me and being together with my family. I felt very confident that everything would work out, and we would again be able to lead a normal life, although I realized that it would be very questionable that I would be able to continue my formal education. While we had a very pleasant and relaxing time in Genoa, we were also anxious to continue our voyage. For me, it was also an adventure going to see a new country and starting a new life.

Finally the day came for us to board the ship. The "Virgilio" was definitely not like the cruise ships of today, but the main thing was it got us safely to our destination. My parents shared a cabin with the parents of my future brother-in-law, Ernst, and I shared a cabin with three Italian women. One of them was very fat. As I did not speak Italian and they did not speak German, I don't think I had any conversation with them. We were lucky to have private cabins with portholes, as a lot of people had to sleep in some kind of steerage, which was actually like a big dormitory without any privacy. The steerage section was below sea level and without air conditioning. Especially when we came to the tropics it was more than uncomfortable. Our cabins were also quite hot, but at least we had fresh air.

Poster of the passenger ship Virgilio

As we had some board money, my parents rented some deck chairs for us right away to make the trip more comfortable. At that time you had to pay for the use of deck chairs. Later when I went from Caracas to New York I had a chair assigned to me, and the steward always carried the chair wherever I wanted to sit. I don't remember if I had to pay for it. Our first port of call was Marseille. I went down from the ship and all I remember of Marseille were warehouses. A lot of new people boarded the ship in Marseille and the ship was really very full. I don't think there was an empty bed to be found anywhere.

As long as we were in the Mediterranean, the sea was nice and smooth, but the minute we passed the Strait of Gibraltar into the Atlantic Ocean, I got very seasick. It lasted, I think, until we reached our next port, Las Palmas, which is in the Canary Islands. We arrived there at night, but I stepped off the boat just to say that I stepped on African soil. I had no more seasickness after Las Palmas. The ship, as one can imagine, was crowded but there weren't any big problems. In general people were happy to be on their way to the unknown, hoping that it would be better than what we had left behind.

It took us ten days to get to La Guaira, Venezuela, our first port in South America. According to information, one evening we passed close to the island of St. Lucia. It was an Italian ship and there were many Italians on board. They started to sing Italian folksongs and many people joined in. It was a nice change from the monotony of the life on the ship, although I don't recall being bored. In La Guaira, we left the ship for some sightseeing and got our first impression of

South America and also of a tropical country. We spent the whole day walking around. It was a good feeling walking again on land, inhaling the air of South America. La Guaira is in the tropics and it was very hot. In spite of not having much money, my mother could not resist and bought a pineapple. In Vienna before the war, pineapples were more or less a luxury. You saw them only in some specialty stores and you might buy a slice, but you never got the real flavor of it. My mother brought the pineapple on the ship and at first she did not want to cut it as she enjoyed so much the aroma of this wonderful fruit. I wanted to see as much as possible of La Guaira as I knew it was unlikely that I would ever return to this place. Little did I know that ten years later I would move to Venezuela and La Guaira and the surroundings would become regular part of our Sunday excursions.

Our next port was Cristóbal at the entrance to the Panama Canal. There I had my first contact with American citizens, as part of Cristóbal and the Panama Canal was then American territory. As I landed in American territory, I saw bilingual English/Spanish newspapers for the first time. Along the waterfront of Cristóbal were many stores, mostly owned by the Japanese, who sold very cheap men's shirts and other things made of silk. My parents bought four of those silk shirts for my father for one U.S. dollar. Although we did not have much money, we did not wanted to miss this opportunity to get such a bargain. I don't believe that my dad ever wore those shirts. I also got a kimono robe, in blue with a big embroidered dragon on the back, also for a dollar. I did not wear this robe much either, because La Paz was much too cold for a silk robe and our first living accommodations were not exactly proper for silk robes. I wore it on my first solo vacation in Cochabamba, but somehow I felt foolish wearing it.

We were supposed to stay overnight in Cristóbal, but because of rumors that some American warships were transferred from the Pacific to the Atlantic, we left in the evening. It was April 1939 and war was in the air. We left Cristóbal late in the evening for the first part of the trip through the Panama Canal. Actually we were very fortunate, to say the least, because to transfer through the Panama Canal during the day is very hot and we did not have air conditioning. It was also very interesting going through the first locks at night where everything was very well lit. We stopped after the first locks and spent the rest of the night at a great lake; at least it looked to me like a lake. Very early the next morning we continued the crossing and there I saw American soldiers, including some black soldiers. They were guarding the canal and the installations. I was very favorably impressed by those soldiers—I was just fifteen—and I thought they were the most wonderful and handsome people in the whole world.[7]

When we left the canal, the color of the Atlantic Ocean suddenly turned gray-blue. Upon leaving the canal we saw hundreds of fish, or perhaps they were dolphins, playing and jumping in the water. At that

---

[7] Years later I wanted to relive the wonderful experience I had in 1939, but it was not the same. First, there were no more American soldiers guarding the canal, and the excitement was gone. I did not enjoy seeing the Panama Canal so much the second time, in spite of having a cabin with air conditioning and every comfort a cruise ship can offer.

time it did not impress me very much as I considered it as part of the landscape, and I looked for them years later when I returned for my second crossing of the Panama Canal, but they were not there. It might be that they are there only at certain times of the year and that I had missed them.

Our next stop was Guayaquil, Ecuador. At that time the harbor was too small for a ship as large as ours to dock in the harbor. People had to leave the ship by small boats called "tenders", which looked to me quite scary. There were a few people from our ship who were immigrating to Ecuador and left the ship. They felt superior to us poor people who had to go to Bolivia. For most of the emigrants on the ship, Bolivia was their final destination. There were some people on the ship who were crossing the Atlantic for a second time. They had first traveled to Uruguay and the country did not let them land there. They had to return to Marseille. They were able to board our ship because they received an entry visa for Bolivia in Marseille.

The next port of call was Callao, the harbor for Lima, the capital of Peru. The port is very close to Lima, like a suburb, and today has nice beaches and hotels. We arrived there on the first of May, which was a national holiday and because of that the harbor was more or less closed. There were no laborers to attend to the ship. We spent two miserable days in Callao; it was very hot and those of us with German passports, which had the letter "J" indicating we were Jewish refugees, were not allowed to go on land. Apparently the government was afraid that people would leave the ship and stay in Peru instead of going to the country for which they had visas.

ON THE WAY TO LA PAZ

Finally, after four weeks on the ship, we approached our port of destination—Arica, Chile. We arrived there late at night and as this harbor was also too small to accommodate our ship, we had to disembark on those small tender boats. It was really very scary as we saw some lights on the horizon, but they looked very far away. The only good thing was that there was a full moon. The boat took off and suddenly the skipper stopped and demanded some money. I don't know how it was settled, but finally around midnight we landed in Arica.

As my future brother-in-law and my sister were already in La Paz, they were able to make reservations for us in a hotel in Arica where we had to spend a few days until we were able to continue our trip to La Paz. The train from Arica to La Paz went only twice weekly. Arica had a very nice big hotel right on the beach and behind the hotel was a very big bald mountain, "El Moro," actually a very big rock. As it never rains in Arica, the mountain does not have any vegetation. At first I did not believe that it never rains there. As I saw that the houses had barely any roofs (the roofs there are more for shade), I started to believe it. A few years later, my parents and my sister went to Arica for a vacation.

As the place where we stayed did not offer any food, we had to provide our own. My mother had known about it when we left Vienna. My parents were not sure if we would have enough money to buy food and how expensive it would be, so my mother brought some cans of sardines from Vienna. That was more or less the only canned food we were familiar with in Austria. For the few days until we were able to board the train for our final destination in La Paz, we lived on our sardines, and some bread, which we had enough money to buy, and bananas.

Finally came the day that we could board the train for La Paz. We boarded the train toward evening. We were told that within a few hours the train would climb to 13,780 feet and that we might have some problems due to the sudden change of the altitude, but really did not know what to expect. There were all kinds of horror stories about altitude sickness, but frankly they are not worth repeating.

A village on the Altiplano

In the morning when we awoke, our view of Bolivia looked very sad. We were on the Altiplano of Bolivia, which is above the tree line. As there is very little rain, it looked like kind of a desert. There were no trees, no grass or greenery and very little vegetation. On the different stops in little villages we saw some houses, which looked like they were made of mud. Actually those adobe houses were quite steady and durable in the harshness of the climate on the Altiplano. We saw the Indian population, with their many colorful skirts and bowler hats and wearing shoes that looked like they were made of old automobile tires.

Toward afternoon we arrived at the train station in the town of Viacha. This was the last train station before descending to La Paz. Its altitude was 13,780 feet above sea level. Actually the train ride from Arica to La Paz can be very depressing if you don't know that at the end you find a nice livable city as I knew from letters Ernst had sent to us. For people who did not know what to expect, the ride during the day on the Altiplano could be very discouraging.

The Altiplano

When we arrived at the Viacha train station we had the very pleasant surprise of being met by Lilly, Ernst and his sister Stella, as they were able to board the train there. Ernst's brother Kurt was not with them, because at that time he was working as a doctor in a tin or silver mine. It was a wonderful reunion.

La Paz itself is in a valley surrounded by mountains over 13,000 feet. The altitude of La Paz on the main square is 11,800 feet above sea level. From the Viacha station, I believe it took more than one hour to make a very winding descent to reach La Paz, our final destination.

La Paz postcard

Ernst made reservations for us in a boarding house belonging to Bolivians. We were glad to have someplace to stay. At the same time, a few hundred people arrived with us and La Paz did not have enough accommodations to house this sudden arrival of people. Also in the Viacha Station, people from a Jewish welfare committee boarded the train and arranged temporary housing for people in some kind of dormitory until everyone could find some proper housing.

Ernst, along with his sister and brother-in-law, had a small boarding house in La Paz where his sister and brother-in-law were in charge of the kitchen. Ernst had learned to bake and to make liquor in Vienna, which helped the success of the boarding house. In La Paz it was very easy to find household help, as well as for help in the kitchen and for cleaning, but you had to instruct the helpers—they mostly followed your instructions. Unfortunately, the partnership did not work out and after a short time everyone went their separate ways.

When we arrived, Lilly was staying in a rented room and it was planned that upon our arrival she and Ernst would get married. Due to the breakup of the partnership, they finally got married one year later, on the day Paris was occupied by the Germans on June 14, 1940. Lilly's English was good enough that she was able to get a job in an office supply store that imported typewriters and other office supplies. This salary helped us a little until we were able to get our "Landungsgeld."

We stayed at the boarding house for only a few days. It was too expensive and we could not tolerate the food. This could also have been due to the change in climate, as it takes a while to acclimate oneself to living at such a high altitude. Temporarily, my parents rented a small room where we could use the kitchen and utensils until we got our own luggage and also our money, which was supposed to be deposited in the Central Bank of Bolivia.

THE CITY OF LA PAZ

Now I will make a little introduction to and description of La Paz. La Paz lays in a kind of a bowl with one exit toward a valley. The altitude of La Paz is between 9,843 feet and 13,123 feet. The main square is about in the middle of the city and is at almost 12,000 feet.

Downtown La Paz, 1938

When I was living in Bolivia, the population was about 3,000,000[8]. The population then was about thirty percent Quechua, living mostly in the lower altitudes; twenty five percent Aymara, living in the Highlands; thirty percent Mestizos; and fifteen percent Caucasian. The Quechuas and the Aymaras had their own languages, but in the cities most of them knew Spanish.

---

[8] Today the population of La Paz is about 1,200,000 and the population of Bolivia about 9,000,000 people.

Due to the altitude and the very dry climate, La Paz and its surroundings have very little vegetation but the mountains have the most beautiful colorful rock formations.

The highlight of La Paz is Mount Illimani. This mountain is 21,325 feet above sea level and always covered with snow or ice and visible from many parts of the city. Actually sometimes it looks as if the city ends on the mountain. When I was married, we had an apartment with a view of the mountain. It was the most beautiful vista I had ever seen. At a certain time of the year when the sun went down behind the mountain, the snow had the color of purple or when the moon rose over the mountain, it took on the color of gold. This might be why I like to visit glaciers so much, as they remind me of Mount Illimani.

As in any Spanish city, La Paz has a main square on which the President's Palace, the Parliament and the main church are located. There was also a hotel and some stores. The houses, except for the government buildings, were very old and mainly built of adobe. The center itself had very steep streets, which made walking difficult due to the reduced oxygen in the very high altitude. A few blocks down from the main square was a street with modern office buildings, primarily occupied by the offices of the mining companies.

Bolivia is very rich in silver and tin mines. Actually, a mountain close to the city of Potosí was declared "Silver Mountain" by the Spanish conquistadors. They extracted much silver from this mountain and even during my stay in Bolivia, this mine was very productive. In the rivers and in the lowland jungles

San Francisco Church in La Paz

you could find gold. During the time I lived there,
three men, who came to be known as the 'Bolivian Tin
Barons,' owned most of the mines. They were: Simón
Iturri Patiño, a Bolivian native; Carlos Victor Aramayo;
and Dr. Moritz (Don Mauricio) Hochschild, a German
agnostic Jew, who greatly helped the new Jewish refugees in resettling.

One part of the city was occupied primarily by
native Indians. The women wore very colorful dresses.
These were composed of many skirts, one over the

other, each one in a different color and topped by colorful serapes and bowler hats. The men also had special clothing, but not as colorful, and they very often wore European clothing. In this area was a very beautiful church built by missionaries. This area stretched up into the highlands. When we traveled there later on, my husband Karl and I found it very interesting to walk around there, looking at the different things they sold as well as food and also the very beautiful handicrafts the Indians made. It was very safe to walk there as the people respected Europeans.

The more prosperous people and Europeans lived in the lower part of the city, which was like a suburb with nice houses. This area was preferred because there was more oxygen and in the gardens you could also find trees and nice flowers.

Parallel to the street with the office building was the main street that Ernst had described in his letters. It was actually the widest street in La Paz. In the center was a pedestrian way. On Sunday mornings the military band played there and people strolled around, showing their new dresses and also their new cars, which cruised around and around. It was like a social meeting place where people gossiped, but this was principally just for Bolivians. On the side of the street were restaurants that on Sunday mornings served beer and the La Paz specialty, Saltenas, which are triangle pastries filled with meat, vegetables and unknown things, and usually very spicy. At the beginning, we had other things to occupy ourselves, but in later years we, too, sometimes met friends there. You must realize that hardly anybody had a telephone in La Paz, so there were certain places where you would meet friends. Later, one of the buildings on this street was converted into a synagogue, where I got married.

As a result of the high elevation of La Paz and due to the lack of oxygen, which it usually takes some time to get used to, everything is done more slowly. This means that if you walked fast you ran out of breath, so you didn't walk too fast. In comparison to other countries in South America, the people in Bolivia also spoke more slowly. Also, due to the lack of oxygen, nothing burned fast. There was not even a fire department in La Paz while I was living there. Even in the cotton mill where Karl worked they had no special precautions for fire and the dust in cotton mills is very flammable. Minor skin cuts needed longer to heal and because of that you were more likely to get an infection. During the early 1940s there were no antibiotics, but somehow with old family recipes everything healed properly, it just took longer.

In spite of the fact that La Paz is located very close to the equator, the nights were very cold, sometimes even reaching the point of frost. During the day the sun was warm, but in the shade it was always cold. Summer is in December and July and August are the winter months. In general, the climate is very dry. The rainy season is during summer. Sometimes it rains during the winter months, when you could find snow on the mountains and the steep streets could be very slippery. You had to walk very carefully, but usually by around 10:00 in the morning the snow and ice would be completely melted.

A VERY DIFFICULT BEGINNING

Our first days and months in La Paz were very challenging, but somehow we did not lose our optimism to succeed. We did not have any other choice than to look forward to better times, because we were very glad to be where we were.

As I mentioned, we had left the boarding house after a few days and rented a small room where we could use the kitchen and utensils, as we had only our suitcases with the clothing we had brought on the trip. My parents bought three beds for us, although bed is probably too good a word. They consisted of three wooden frames with mattresses filled with straw and covered with some jute material. They were rustic, but frankly I slept very well on those primitive beds until a few years later when my parents could afford to buy real beds with proper mattresses.

As soon as we arrived in La Paz, my father went to the National Bank of Bolivia to get our money but unfortunately we found out that the Consul of Bolivia in Genoa did not transfer the money, as he was required to do. Later we discovered that he did this with other people's money, too. Here we were, with no money, our crates hopefully somewhere on the way. When they did arrive we would definitely not have the money to get them out of customs. There was an organization that worked to help Jewish refugees in La Paz called the Hebrew Immigrant Aid Society that worked in partnership with the American Joint Distribution Committee. My father went to this office and they promised to send a cable to Genoa and in a few days we would have the money. This sounded reasonable, but unfortunately it was not so. This was actually the most difficult time we had during the whole emigration and resettlement. The Joint Distribution Committee gave us some money each week for surviving, but it was so minimal that we did not have enough money to buy the most necessary food. As we did not have any valuable things with us, we had nothing to sell. We were afraid to carry any valuables while crossing the German border because if the German police found anything of value we would have been in big trouble. We had forgotten this and packed some silver dessert spoons. My parents said if there were any trouble, we would just throw the spoons out of the window. My parents never realized how dangerous it was to carry anything valuable. We were lucky that we did not have any inspection on the German-Italian border. So we had only the few silver dessert spoons, which we were able to sell, but this did not help very much. My mother even sold her wedding ring. As soon as my father was working again and had some income, it was the first thing that my father replaced, but you must consider what a very emotional thing it was for my mother to sell her ring. As I recall, it took about two months until we got finally our money.

When we arrived in Bolivia, it was a developing country and whatever knowledge you had, even if it was not perfect, could be used to make some income. In the basement where we had this rented room was a small establishment that produced some machine-knitted articles. As I had gone to textile school in Vienna, I tried to get a job there and was hired. After working there for only one day I became sick and had to quit the job. I believe my sickness was mainly due to the fact that I was not used to the altitude and the basement was not very well ventilated.

As we definitely could not afford rent for two rooms and the room where we were staying was very small, my parents were able to find a bigger room, which we sublet from another refugee. He had rented the whole floor in a house and to save on rent he leased two rooms he did not need, one to us and one to another couple. He promised us that until our own crates arrived, he would lend us dishes and other things we needed. Although it was quite a big room, the big disadvantage was that it was located on a steep hill and at this altitude every hill, even if not steep, made you short of breath. It took us quite a while to get used to those hills. So we moved and hired some Indians who carried the beds and our other belongings to our new home. My parents did not buy a fourth bed for my sister, because it was assumed that she would get married very soon. In the meantime, we put the three beds together and I slept between my mother and my sister for nearly one year.

In this first home in La Paz our landlord was an electrician and my mother bought an electric stove from him. Actually, it consisted of two hot plates; each one had two settings, high and low. If you would see this now you would wonder how someone could prepare a meal on such a contraption, but my mother did. You have to consider that in La Paz due to the altitude cooking was much more difficult as everything needed double cooking time to be edible. The boiling point for water in this altitude was 80 Celsius or 176 Fahrenheit (normal boiling temperature for water on sea level is 212 Fahrenheit). We were still better off than other people with their cooking utensils, as many people cooked on Primus cookers, which are actually used as camping equipment. The cooking plates my mother used had coils, which sometimes broke. Then my mother had to tie them together and when they were broken too often the coils had to be replaced.

I think it was because Lilly had a job that we could afford to pay rent for this room. It had a small additional room adjacent to it, but we did not have need for it as we had so few things. Our furniture consisted of boxes that Lilly could bring from the office. The company where Lilly worked imported typewriters, which came in very sturdy boxes on which my mother could set up the electric stove. She also used some boxes for a table and later when we had our own things she could store dishes and pots there, as the crates had compartments. When finally my parents could buy some furniture I think the first thing my parents acquired was a table with chairs.

Shortly after we moved, the Joint Distribution Committee found a job for me taking care of a small girl in a Bolivian household. The parents wanted the child to learn German. It might have been that they were of German descent, but I don't recall if they spoke German or Spanish to me. My Spanish at that time was very poor. The girl was under two years old and in Bolivia a maid, even one who takes care of children, is not treated as nicely as here in the States and I definitely did not eat with the family. After just a few days my employers, who had some farms or ranches in the interior, decided to leave La Paz to spend some time on those properties and did not need me. That was the end of my being a nursemaid.

Shortly after I returned home my parents finally got the money and we were able to retrieve the crates we sent from Vienna. My father was able to rent a room as a workshop downtown. It was very well located around the corner from the post office and one block from the main square of La Paz. The room my father rented was in a typical old building. On the ground floor were three stores—one was occupied by German refugees as a grocery. It was one of two grocery stores in La Paz owned by refugees, where we were able to buy groceries we were familiar with from Europe. The store carried some food prepared by other refugees, such as sausages, pastries, noodles and bread. The other store was a restaurant owned by a Viennese couple. They had a daughter my age and we later became friends. There was also a third store, but I don't recall what merchandise they had.

From the entrance to the building itself, you walked through a big door and a few steps up and came to a patio. Around the patio were different rooms that were occupied by different refugees as workshops—one was a cobbler and one was an electrician. Those rooms had no windows and the only light they had was by leaving the door open. The room that my father rented faced the street with a big window, and had also a small entrance room. For my father it was very important to have light to work, so it worked well for him. The building had a second floor and there was kind of a veranda with windows around the patio. It had three rooms facing the street. The biggest room facing the street had two doors leading to a small balcony and at the time my father leased his workshop, it was used as a synagogue. The other rooms around the patio were occupied by other families and did not have any windows.

It was assumed that as soon as we retrieved the crates from the custom house and had them delivered to our residence that we would unpack everything and my father take his tools to the place he had rented and then begin looking for work. Unfortunately, it did not go as we had planned. When we opened the crates we realized that all the tools, the motor, etc. were missing—the only thing left was my father's workbench. Later we found out that the permit my father had to take his tools out was revoked. I don't know why, but as my father had to leave Vienna on a certain day we were not able to wait until our things were shipped and so we had to trust the dispatcher. After our inquiry the dispatcher wrote to us that he had everything stored and at a later date if we sent him the money, he would request a new exit permit and forward everything.

That was at the end of July and a few weeks later the war broke out and we never found out what happened to the things. After the war, the dispatcher wrote us that his warehouse was bombed and everything in it destroyed. By the end of the war my father was able to replace most of what was lost. There was only one thing that bothered my parents very much. As one was unable to take any valuable objects out of Germany, my father devised a way to evade the restrictions. He had a small motor similar to a motor dentists used, which he used for his work. This motor had openings all around with the middle completely invisible from the outside. It was in the middle of the motor that my father had hidden my mother's jewels.

As I mentioned before, whatever knowledge or profession you had in Europe you could find work in Bolivia and whatever you were able to produce, you could find some customers. The biggest problems were to get raw materials and tools to work with. As my father had lost all of his tools, we were very worried whether he would be able to replace them. But he found a small store that had supplies for dentists. Tools for jewelers are very similar to those that dentists use. There, my father could buy different pliers and files, and even a dental motor. He was also very lucky that the store had two presses, which my father needed to be able to make sheets or wires when the gold is melted and is soft. In Vienna, my father had a supplier where he could buy gold sheets in different thicknesses and also any kind of wire he would need. In Bolivia this was not available, so my father had to prepare everything himself. It was good fortune that we found those presses.

The next problems were to find someplace where they could prepare one of the presses and make certain grooves to be able to make different sizes of wire. Here we were also lucky, as we found a foundry where they told us that they were able to do this work. It was good that I did not have a job and, as I spoke a little Spanish, I could explain what my father wanted to be done. My knowledge of Spanish consisted mainly of what I had learned from a book we had brought from Vienna and I studied on the ship. Although beginning language books often have phrases that are not useful, it was of some help. I also carried a dictionary with me.

We took the press over to the foundry and my father made some drawings and showed the owner what we would like him to do. The owner was very enthusiastic and promised us to have it finished within three days. My father was very happy that the work would be done as fast as he said—even in Vienna it would have taken much longer to do this kind of job. But at this time we did not know the word "mañana," which can mean a week or a month later. We showed up three days later and he had not even started with the work. Later we found out that he mostly did the work when we were there watching him doing it. It took a couple of months until it was finished, but finally he did a good job and my father was very happy with the results.

The room my father had rented was around the corner from the main post office of La Paz. As nobody had any permanent address, everybody's mail was delivered "Post Restante," which meant when you identified yourself you could pick up the mail that was addressed to your name. As there was no daily train service to La Paz, and no airmail, we depended on the mail delivered by train twice weekly. On those days, people came to the post office—usually it was one member of the family who went to look for mail. At the same time you met people you knew from your ship or other friends you had made. It became a kind of meeting place, as nobody had a telephone, very few had a radio and hardly anybody could afford to buy a newspaper. Besides, most people did not understand enough Spanish to be able to read them anyway, so this was an occasion to get the latest world news and any other information that could be very helpful. As long as I lived in Bolivia and also in Venezuela I never had a telephone. Although most offices in La Paz had a phone, very few people had them in their home. In Caracas many people had telephones, but it was expensive to have one installed. In Caracas I had very friendly neighbors and when I was living alone they offered me the use of their phone any time of the day. Later, when I was working, I used the telephone very often in the office.

After a few weeks nearly everybody had some living accommodations and was busy trying to find a way to support themselves in their new country, so people went their own ways. As the Joint Distribution Committee was located next to Plaza Murillo, most new arrivals at first met there so you always knew when a ship arrived in Chile, because than you saw many new faces on Plaza Murillo and also heard the latest news from Europe, which was often very disturbing.

Many people arrived in Bolivia with visas to be farmers. To help them fulfill their commitment, the Joint Distribution Committee purchased some land in the interior, not too far from La Paz, in an area of lower altitude with potentially more fertile soil, where farms existed before. Hardly any of these new immigrants knew much about cultivating land, and, on top of it, this type of farming was very challenging.

Farming in the tropics was very different than in Europe. It was not very successful and slowly the people drifted back to La Paz or Cochabamba, the second biggest city of Bolivia, to find different ways to

Plaza Murillo, La Paz

support themselves. As many people could not acclimatize themselves to the altitude of La Paz, they moved to Cochabamba, which is only 8,858 feet above sea level with a more temperate climate. The nights there were not so cold and the climate is more like European spring the whole year. Some refugees opened boarding houses in Cochabamba and later we used to go there for vacations.

In general people, including my family, considered Bolivia more or less a transitional place until we could settle somewhere else, but for the time being it was heaven, especially when the war broke out. I will always be thankful and never forget that Bolivia gave us a place to live peacefully and where we were able to support ourselves and live a decent peaceful life. One reason why we did not consider Bolivia as a permanent home was the high altitude, which affected Europeans in many different ways. First, it was very hard on your heart, blood circulation and lungs. For instance babies born to European mothers had a much lower birth weight and also developed much slower than babies born on sea level, although in general they would catch up after awhile. Some people moved even during the war years to Argentina or Chile. After the war when the world situation became more stable, many people left Bolivia. My husband and I left for Venezuela. Kurt Mautner, my brother-in-law, and his family went to Uruguay, as many of his friends went there, too. In later years my parents and my sister moved to New York.

During the time I helped my father to set up his shop, I also tried to find some work for myself. Very close to where my father was going to have his atelier was a knitting mill. I think they had about twenty knitting machines, which were not automatic, but labor in Bolivia was very cheap. I was hired there as a designer. I was actually quite successful there designing some children's clothing, especially little girl's dresses, which were in demand and easy to sell. My success was short-lived though, as it was not long before Germany invaded Poland on September 1, 1939 and World War II began. After a few days, the owner of the knitting mill, who was a German, told me that because of the war he could not get raw materials and dismissed me. I don't know if this was true or if he did not want to have a Jewish employee.

The beginning of the war was a moment I will never forget. There I was in the factory and suddenly all the sirens from the different factories were blowing and at the same time you heard church bells ringing. Whatever could make a noise made a noise and everybody went to the streets to find out what was going on. You have to realize that hardly anybody had a phone and radios were also very rare for us refugees, so that was how you were informed about big world events. In later years the sirens were also active when Paris fell, which I especially remember as it was the day of my sister's wedding. They also sounded during the attack on Pearl Harbor, the beginning of the invasion of Europe, the end of the war in Europe and then, later, the end of the war in Asia, but by that time we all had radios, and didn't depend on the sirens.

Around that time I received a letter from an old school friend from the textile school. He was writing to tell me that he had gone with the Kindertransport to England. He apparently knew that I was in Bolivia from a girlfriend with whom we had gone to school and who was also in England. She left Vienna about the same time I left for Bolivia, but I never heard from her. This friend wrote me that he was continuing to go to school and that he had the measles and wondering which school I was going to. I found this very strange and childish. Here I was trying to find some work to help my parents and he was complaining about his measles. I never answered him and sometimes when I think about it I feel sorry—probably he felt very lonely and homesick and would have liked to get a friendly letter, but I felt too grownup to answer him.

With this job gone and desperately wanting a job in the textile industry, I found out that La Paz had three textile mills. One was for cotton and two were for wool. As textile mills were not built on main streets, I found one that I could reach by streetcar and some walking. Incidentally, the streetcars were actually old cable cars from San Francisco, California. I believe that those in La Paz were either surplus or were those that had been replaced by more modern ones in San Francisco. They worked very well in La Paz on those steep streets.

I was glad to be hired in one of the mills, although it was in an apprentice position. I assumed that in time I would advance and get a job more becoming for a European. I did not stay long in this job, however, as I got really sick and thus never found out if I would have been promoted. It had been very difficult for me to get to the mill; I had to get up very early, as I had to go down the hill where we lived, then go on the streetcar, and then walk up another hill. I believe this was too much for me in this altitude, as apparently I was not completely acclimatized. I was very skinny at that time and had suddenly grown much taller. My illness started with a very bad cough and fever, and as I had been exposed to Indians at the textile mill, my parents thought I had contracted tuberculosis.

My mother took me to a refugee doctor. She was able to practice medicine without official authorization as in Bolivia nobody worried about it. The first thing she said was that I had to gain weight and that I needed vitamins. That was the first time we had heard about vitamins. We had to figure out how to increase the vitamins I was getting, which was not easy in La Paz. We had no fresh milk, only condensed or powdered milk. The only fruit we ate—due to the danger of typhoid fever—had to be peeled or boiled. This meant no lettuce of any kind. We even peeled tomatoes. But bananas and oranges and pineapples were excellent and we ate a lot of them. Native tropical fruits like mangos, papayas, avocados were unknown to us and at first we were afraid to eat them.

In Bolivia in the late 1930s vitamins were very expensive so the doctor suggested I should eat one pound of grapes daily, as that was the time of the year when you could get grapes at the market. However, this was not such an easy suggestion. How could you peel grapes? What you could do, and my mother did, was the following. First, she rinsed the grapes with boiled but still hot water, then soaked the grapes for about twenty minutes in a solution of permanganate—this was a purple powder—and then rinsed the grapes again with cold water that was boiled before. So eating grapes in La Paz was a big project. For each pound of grapes one needed four pots of boiled water. On top of it, the stove my mother used was not always very reliable. Because of the altitude, you had to let the water boil for about ten minutes to be germ free. Later on we ate boiled grapes, which were very good and tasty. We did the same with strawberries. Besides not having milk, and because with the exception of sardines, we had no fish, the doctor suggested that I have some calcium tablets, which we could afford.

There was no fresh fish in La Paz, as at that altitude there were no rivers. The only supply of fresh fish was from Lake Titicaca—and the fish from there were like big sardines with lots of bones. Once a week a train from the coastal city of Antofagasta, Chile sometimes brought fish; but as there was no refrigeration we were not sure that the fish were fresh. In later years, there was refrigeration, and occasionally we were able to get some fish.

LIFE IS IMPROVING

In the building where my father had his work-shop, the big front room on the second floor was used as a synagogue. My father found out that the synagogue was moving to a bigger place and was able to rent this room for us. As we were living on a very steep hill and it was very exhausting to get there, we were very glad to be able to rent this room. It was especially convenient for my father. When we had already paid rent for this room and wanted to move, the Rabbi or whoever was in charge asked my father if we could delay our move so that they could still lead a Sabbath service there and bless the room for us. My father agreed and we always said that this little gesture brought us luck, as from then on my father always had plenty of orders and became successful in his profess-sion in Bolivia.

For the move, we again hired some Indians, who walked in a column carrying our beds and belong-ings. It was not an unusual sight in La Paz to see this method of moving. We did not know if moving vans existed at that time. For later moves, we usually rented a truck.

When I look back at our living quarters at that time, I only have to say that we were satisfied with very little. We had only one room, although it was a very big room. It was not what I was used to having in Vienna, where I had my own bedroom, as did my sister and my parents. Naturally we had a bathroom, kitchen and living room. At the beginning in La Paz, my mother cooked in that room until later when we were able to rent an adjacent room, but I was very happy there. The bathroom was used by everyone who lived on the same floor. I believe we were about one dozen people sharing the bathroom. The most important thing was that I felt secure and far away from the war, although not in our wildest dreams could we imagine what really was going on in Europe.

Shortly after our move, my coughing improved. I recovered completely and for the rest of the time that I lived in La Paz I never had any serious sickness. With regard to health in general, one had to be very careful. You could never drink the water; it always had to be boiled, even for brushing teeth. We drank very little water—mostly we had tea. We did not know about dehydration. There were some kinds of bottled soft drinks available, but we definitely could not afford them. In later years the Coca-Cola Company built a plant in La Paz. As long as I was living in South America I never drank water from the faucet.[9]

During the first year when we were living in La Paz, a few people caught typhoid fever. My brother-in-law, Kurt Mautner, had it and survived, but some people did not. Later, every year we were inoculated against typhoid fever. Those injections were quite painful. We usually had them done on weekends, since they could also cause a high fever and it took a couple of days to be able to recover. After a few years, our

_____

[9] When I came to the States it took me a long time until I felt comfortable drinking water straight from the faucet. In the beginning when I was living in the States, I first put a bottle filled with water into the refrigerator and then I drank it. Even today, with exception of brushing my teeth, I hardly ever use the water in the bathroom for drinking.

bodies apparently had enough antibodies, so it was not too bad anymore.

After I recovered from my cough, I found a job in a very small knitting factory. It belonged to two men from Poland and they needed someone to watch the workers and check the finished sweaters for imperfecttions for sale. Even before the war, we were able to sell everything; later during the war there was a shortage of many finished products, as much could not be imported. This was especially true when the United States entered the war. Whatever you were able to produce, there was a market for it. I stayed on this job quite a while, at least more than one year. The shortage of imported merchandise also helped us newcomers to establish ourselves, as nearly everybody had the so-called "Landungsgeld," which was required to obtain a visa to get to Bolivia. Because labor was cheap, you were able to start a business with little money. Some people opened restaurants, pastry shops and boarding houses, as newcomers had to live somewhere. If you had some knowledge of any kind of profession, like as a seamstress, tailor, or electrician, etc., you found work.

In La Paz ready-made clothing was not available; you had to have everything made to order, even shoes. I ordered mine from a shoemaker. He was a Bolivian, and I chose a shoe model from a catalogue, selected the leather and always got very nice good-fitting shoes. At the beginning it was more difficult for white-collar workers to establish themselves—for instance, lawyers—but some were able to open some retail stores or found jobs in existing offices. Some tried to start businesses importing merchandise from other countries, mostly in South America. When the United States and Japan entered the war, imports, especially from Japan, were no longer available and those from the United States were very limited. Some people opened offices as representatives of foreign countries as my brother-in-law Kurt Mautner did.

Dr. Moritz (Don Mauricio) Hochschild was a German Jew who had been in Bolivia for many years and had become very wealthy and influential as the owner of several tin mines. He had recently opened a new modern hotel which needed many workers. He was a big help in providing jobs for refugees. He hired people and trained them for the different departments. He also hired people for working in his offices or to work at the mines. After the partnership of Ernst with his sister Stella was dissolved, Ernst started to work at Dr. Hochschild's hotel. The jobs at the mines were very well paid, but the locations of the mines were at a very high altitude (more than 13,000 feet). The living conditions were very primitive and the cold climate, due to the elevation, was very difficult for Europeans. Many of those working at the mines later tried to get transferred to La Paz or left the company. Kurt Grab, the brother of my brother-in-law, was working as a physician at a mine in Potosí, but left for health reasons. He was then hired by the Bolivian Government to work at a little outpost on the border between Bolivia and Brazil. His experiences there are another story, which I will mention later.

As we all started more or less with nothing, everybody tried to help everybody and there was no jealousy. With time people became more successful. Groups and clubs were formed and you found your own circle where you felt comfortable. One big thing was that in general the emigrants did not integrate with the Bolivian population. This was partly because the so-called society did not accept us and the middle class was very small and in part because we had nothing in common with the Indian population. Every nationality had their own club—the British, American, Swiss, etc.—so we newly-arrived Austrian Jews started our own club as well.

There was a club of Eastern European Jews; they had their own building and also a synagogue in the same building. Those people had mostly arrived in Bolivia during the 1920s and 1930s. Some helped us newcomers to establish ourselves, but we formed our own circle of friends and clubs. The Austrian Club was very big for both my parents and myself. The president of this club, Mr. Terramare, was a former director of a Vienna theater and his wife was a former actress. She later opened a jewelry store and my father worked very much with her. Mr. Terramare occasionally organized theater performances with his wife and some very good amateur actors. Naturally every German-speaking person went to those performances and we enjoyed it so much, as there were often sketches of current events and different personalities. There were many young people about my age and we founded a Jewish Club, named Maccabi, where we met for different social affairs. The club was in the basement of the synagogue. Much later we had our own tennis courts.

As there were many people with young children, the emigrants opened a school for the children. However, I was too old for this kind of school. Slowly nearly everybody got adjusted to the altitude and life in

Bolivia and most people found ways to support themselves. Life became somewhat normal, but we were still clinging to our European customs, such as our food habits, as much as possible.

Slowly we could also afford some luxuries, like going to a movie or buying ice cream. There was a store owned by refugees that sold ice cream. As an electric refrigerator was unknown to us, ice cream was something very special. In La Paz, as well as in Caracas, going to a movie meant really going out. You dressed up for it, especially on Thursdays, and also on Sundays when the new releases were shown. People bought new hats for those performances and you really put on your finery—it was something special. Sometimes on Sunday afternoons, we went to a suburb called Obrajes, which was in a valley at a lower elevation than La Paz and had trees and, because of this, had more oxygen. We were able to reach it by bus, and enjoyed some time in the garden restaurants there, which were similar to beer gardens.

As a lot of people came to Bolivia with a visa for agriculture, of those one family built a kind of hacienda and farm, which was very close to La Paz and could easily be reached by taxi. Taxi rides were very cheap and affordable to us. I frequently went there on Sundays with my parents. Sometimes we had lunch or afternoon coffee. My parents met friends and as the war was going on they discussed whatever one knew about the war, which was actually very limited. At first, they discussed the war in Europe and later it included the war in the Pacific. As soon as my parents could afford it, they bought a shortwave radio and most Sundays at five o'clock we were home to listen to the news in the German language, from London. Later during the war with Japan, we had some problems understanding what was going on as we had little knowledge of the geography of the Orient. On the farm, I met people my own age and especially enjoyed the visits there because of that.

As our financial situation improved, my parents slowly bought decent furniture. Our two rooms were furnished with all the essentials, except my mother still used the contraption for cooking and only much later when my parents had a very nice apartment did my mother get a proper stove. As hardly anybody had a telephone, visits were very casual; you just knocked on the door and you were always welcome. My brother-in-law Ernst had a cousin, Walter Freud, with whom we had traveled on the ship to Bolivia. Walter had a job at the Hotel Sucre and some time off in the evenings. Every evening at eight o'clock there was a knock on our door and there was Walter. Later, when we had a radio, he and my parents listened to music. There was a radio station with classical music, which sometimes played Viennese music, which my father especially enjoyed. We all had tea together and a couple of hours later Walter would leave to go back to his job.

Very close to where we lived was an emigrant who apparently brought many German books from Germany and perhaps bought German books from other refugees. He opened a library where I could rent books. As in Vienna, my reading material was mostly books proper for children and teens. Here I had the opportunity to get books for my own age and the owner of the library recommended books to me, which I really enjoyed. Some were modern; some were classics, although many German classics I had already read in school in Vienna. Among many books I read, I especially remember <u>Tom Sawyer</u> by Mark Twain in German. Later in Caracas I read it in Spanish and finally, not too long ago, I read it in English. Usually I sat in a corner and never was disturbed by the talks my parents had with Walter or other visitors, as I was not interested in their conversations.

Even in Vienna I had a love for tennis, and as soon as I could afford it, around the beginning of 1940, I joined the Maccabi Tennis Club in La Paz. I bought a tennis racquet then—I still have it, but when I look at it now it looks more like an antique, which it is, as it is about seventy years old. Considering the altitude, you never played longer than one set; also when I took lessons, one never played more than one set, or have a lesson longer than half an hour. I never became a champion, but I liked tennis very much and later played it in Caracas, too. I still enjoy watching the big tennis tournaments.

After about a year and a half working in the knitting factory, I believe it was during 1941, I was offered a job by the owner of a store that made and sold hats to come to her store and learn the profession of milliner. As hats were very much in demand, and my parents no longer depended on my salary, I decided to take the new job in order to learn a new profession, despite the smaller salary.

My father's success in La Paz was due to the fact that he was exceptional in his profession, and able to make his own designs. Because of a big inflation of the Bolivar, which is the national currency, as soon as people could afford it they liked to invest in gold jewelry, sometimes to replace what they had lost due to the emigration from Europe. Many considered gold the most secure investment. Although in Vienna my father had mostly worked in platinum in settings that required many diamonds and other fine stones, in Bolivia, he worked exclusively in gold and he specialized in jewelry with Indian motifs, which he designed, and had a Bolivian engraver follow his designs.

A short time after my father opened his store; he received a big order from the Bolivian government. The president of Bolivia and the president of Argentina were meeting at the Bolivia-Argentina border to open a new railroad connection between those two countries and my father had the contract to make commemorative medals in gold for the dignitaries who attended this meeting. There was a very interesting byline to this order. In Bolivia gold was not officially sold on the open market. The government gave my father the gold for the work. When my father looked at the pieces of gold he received for the work, he recognized it as some antiques and showed those pieces to us. Some looked like breast shields and some like cufflinks. My father very reluctantly melted those pieces, but he did not have any other choice. A few years ago, when I was at the Metropolitan Museum in New York, I saw Inca cufflinks, like those my father melted for the medals. What a shame that he was not able to keep them, as they were really very valuable antiques.

In general my father purchased gold from Indians, which sometimes was from mines but mostly found in rivers in the jungle, toward the East side of Bolivia, toward the Brazilian border. As those gold flakes were not pure and contained other minerals, my father had to eliminate those foreign materials with some very dangerous acids and added silver or copper according to the shade of color he wanted so it became 18 karats, which was the desired gold in South America.

LIFE IMPROVES

Due to the altitude, everyone tried to get away from La Paz to a lower altitude to relax from the cold and harsh climate. While living in La Paz, I was never able to leave the house without a coat. The nights were especially cold. During the day the sun was very warm —after all we were living very close to the equator— but in the shade it was always chilly. The heating system we used was also very primitive. As soon as we could afford it we bought an electric stove and when you sat in front of it one felt warm, but it did not heat the room very well, so we always wore sweaters.

My parents went the first time for a vacation to Cochabamba, which is only 9,186 feet above sea level, sometime during 1942. Many refugees had moved to Cochabamba partly because they could not tolerate the altitude of La Paz and partly because Cochabamba had a spring-like climate year round, with blooming flowers and trees and greenery.

After my parents returned, they suggested I should go too. In Cochabamba were a couple of pensions, or boarding houses. I stayed in one owned by refugees. To go from La Paz to Cochabamba was a very long train ride. You left early in the morning, went across the Altiplano to Oruro, a mining town, and in the afternoon the train slowly descended into a lower altitude where you suddenly saw vegetation. As long as you were on the Altiplano it was very dusty as there was very little vegetation at that altitude. You could see on the far horizon snow-covered mountains, but they were very far away. I ate lunch in the dining car and felt very grown up. Shortly before I left for my vacation, Coca-Cola opened a branch in La Paz and I had my first taste of Coca-Cola on the train ride. As they served the drink warm, I did not like it. I believe because of this, I still don't like Coca-Cola.

My brother-in-law Ernst and his brother Kurt's parents lived in Cochabamba, so I was not alone and had somebody to visit. The boarding house was on the outskirts of Cochabamba and there was a train going downtown. The trains had open wagons, like in some resorts, which are called elephant trains and were very pleasant to ride, especially in a warm climate.

Ernst's brother, Kurt, was a physician. When he arrived in Bolivia he got a job as a physician for a mining company, but among other things, the climate did not agree with him—after all, the location of the mine was over 13,000 feet. When he returned from the mine, the government offered him a job at a military outpost in the jungle close to the border of Brazil. The outpost was supposed to be supplied by the government with all necessities like food, ammunition, medicines, etc. But in many parts of South America everything is "mañana" and the supply of food was less than adequate. According to Kurt, they had plenty of bananas, but meat was another story and being in the jungle they had to hunt for their own supply. Living in Vienna he never had a rifle in his hand and definitely was not a very good hunter. He told us some very funny stories. The only animals he could shoot were parrots—but not the young ones, who were able to fly away from him. The only ones he could get were very old ones and the meat was hardly edible. They had a limited amount of ammunition and could not waste anything. The natives, according to his stories, were very good hunters and as the jungle is full of all kinds of animals, he consumed meat as a European he never thought he would eat. The natives liked to hunt for monkeys and prepare the whole monkey and bring it skinned to the table. I am sure you can imagine how a whole cooked monkey looked; it definitely took his appetite away. After awhile he had enough of this adventure and returned to Cochabamba, where he lived with his parents and practiced medicine illegally, as he did not have a license. In the late 1940s he moved to Boston and practiced as a psychologist. He died in Boston in the 1980s.

In the boarding house, for the first time in my life I was treated like a grown up. I was sharing the same table in the dining room with a chemist or biologist, who lived in Santa Cruz, a town east of the Andes in a very low altitude and a very hot tropical climate. He worked in a laboratory, which retrieved poison from snakes to be converted into serum to be used against snakebites. He explained to me in great detail how it was done and in spite of explaining it to me during a meal, it did not take away my appetite. I must have found it very interesting, because I still clearly remember about the procedure, which can be very dangerous.

While I was in Cochabamba, I received a letter from my boyfriend in which he spelled the name of Cochabamba incorrectly. To be honest, the whole letter was nothing to brag about. After I returned from the vacation, my mother made very clear to me that my father was not very happy with this friendship of mine, but by this time I had already come to my own conclusion to end this friendship. My old boyfriend was very much against me improving myself—and that was also one thing I did not like about him.

My parents were sorry that I was unable to finish my education and arranged with a German refugee to teach me English—with a good German accent. They felt it was important for me to learn English as they hoped someday to move to the United States. As I have already mentioned and can't emphasize enough, we were very grateful and happy to be able to live in Bolivia, although we considered it more or less as a transitional place. Mostly due to the altitude, we did not consider it a permanent home. Then, too, we were always considered immigrants and our children as children of immigrants. During the time I was living in La Paz, there was hardly any intermarriage between Jewish immigrants and Bolivians.

When I returned from Cochabamba, I changed from my job with Mrs. Frischer, the milliner, to working with Jenny Lowy, who also had a company that made high-quality hats. It was not an open store; it was located in a residential area, where she also lived with her husband and her mother who both also helped with the work. It was a very pleasant working place. While I was working there Jenny was expecting a baby and we all felt like a family expecting our niece or nephew. I don't know if it was because Jenny was pregnant and she had a craving for it, but every afternoon her mother served us liverwurst sandwiches. At first I liked them very much, but after a while I got tired of liverwurst and would have liked a change. To this day, if I see liverwurst, I can still taste those sandwiches, and now I eat them only occasionally.

All the employees admired Jenny very much. Not only was she very good looking and a very pleasant person to be with, but I also considered her to be very bright. As I mentioned, working at Jenny's was very pleasant and we girls were also friends outside of the workplace. Sometimes we went together to the movies or to an afternoon tea to the Hotel Sucre to dance.

Most Sunday mornings I went to play tennis at our Maccabi courts, and sometimes was also able to take time off from work during the week to take tennis lessons since the courts were very close to where I worked. Apparently I did not take enough lessons, because I never became a very good player, but I enjoyed it very much.

After working for Jenny for about one year, I went again to Cochabamba and stayed at the same boarding house. This time there were also some bachelor guests. Those young men were working in different mines, belonging mostly to Dr. Hochschild. The salaries at those mines were relatively very good. Not having any way to spend money in the mines and being deprived of any entertainment and also of decent food, they tried to catch up in every way. There were also some young couples there and they invited me to join them when they went out in the evening downtown. I had a very good time on this trip, as I felt like I was being treated as an adult for the very first time. I had my first taste of whiskey on that trip. I did not enjoy it, but did find that gin mixed with a lot of ginger ale was more to my liking. There were no occasions to get drunk. We went to some nightclubs or bars where you listened to music and danced and we mostly had a lot of conversations and laughs. One has to realize that buying records in Bolivia during the war was a problem; they were just not available, so listening to records was something special. In general when we went downtown, all the guests in the boarding house joined, with the exception of one couple. I was told that they had lost a baby due to negligence in the hospital, so they did not feel like celebrating. I did not pay much attention in regard to this couple. In a twist of fate, this couple came to play a significant role in my life just a few months later.

KARL MAUTNER
ENTERS MY LIFE

Shortly after I returned from Cochabamba, my parents wanted to go with me to the Hotel Sucre for the Sunday five o'clock tea. I don't know if it was due to bad weather and my parents did not feel like going to the Finca as it was usual their custom, or whether the news from England was not of special interest, anyway we went together to the dance.

In La Paz it was very common that parents or mothers went with their daughters to those teas, but young men went usually with some friends. I had been a few times at those teas with some girlfriends. On this special Sunday, Karl Mautner, with his friend Heinz Frankenstein, where there too. Both were competing to dance with me. Apparently, Karl won and he invited me to go a movie with him the following week. So, in March of 1944 my life with Karl began.

As Karl became part of my life, I think it is important to describe his background.

Karl's father, Gustav Mautner, was born in Jicin, Czechoslovakia, and died in Vienna, in February of 1938. He married Gertrude Schnitzler who was born in August 1888 and died in August 1947 in La Paz. She was born in a town on the border between Germany and Czechoslovakia, in what was called Sudetenland, close to Dresden, Germany.

They married in 1907 and had two sons. Kurt was born April 1908 in Vienna and died October 1970 in London. Karl was born February 1918 in Vienna, and died in La Guaira, Venezuela, on December 21, 1952.

Gustav had several brothers; all were involved in one way or another in the textile industry. Most of the family lived in Czechoslovakia, and as far as I know, they escaped to England before the war.

Gertrude had one stepsister; her father was a widower and married a second time. The stepsister's name was Helene. She married a man named Bauer and they also lived in Vienna and had a store for stamp collectors. I was told that the Bauer's had a son who passed away shortly before Germany occupied Austria. However, when Hitler came, they moved to Czechoslovakia with the stepmother, and all of them were sent to Theresienstadt concentration camp. According to Karl's mother the relationship between the mother and stepdaughter was not too good, but she took good care of the mother and had to prepare her for the trip to Auschwitz, where she died. The Bauer's survived Theresienstadt and after the war, they settled in Prague where they lived quietly until they passed away.

After Karl finished a technical school, he started to work for a cousin in one of the Mautner family's two textile mills. One was in Koenighof, Czechoslovakia; the other close to Vienna, about two hours by bus or train, close to the province of Burgenland. After Karl finished technical school, he actually did not want to get into the textile business, but there was a saying, "whichever way a Mautner goes, he always ends up somehow connected to the textile industry." His father had a business for spare parts for the textile industry. That was okay for the generation of Karl and Kurt and their cousins, but the next generation—that of my son Willy and Kurt's son Ernesto and grand-sons—have had nothing to do with the textile industry.

Textile mills are usually not built on a town's main street. This was true for the new mill where Karl started to work, which was in a very remote place—not the most interesting place for a young man to live and work. He was able to come home on weekends to Vienna by bus, where he continued his studies at the Vienna Textile School, but with travel time, there was not much time for social activities. It was not a happy time for him.

When Hitler occupied Vienna in March of 1938, all plans for the future became obsolete. With the death of his father Gustav, Kurt was supposed to take over the business. However, because of the new Nazi laws, this was not possible, and an employee took over the firm. According to what I was told, this arrangement was supposed to be only temporary, and was done in a friendly way. They were forced to sell the house, which they owned and in which they lived, for a price the government set and the family was forced to move to an apartment. The factory was also confiscated by the government.

The brothers were able to get entry visas for Bolivia, and they left Vienna during July of 1938, with the thought that after settling in Bolivia, their mother should follow. While on the ship, the brothers met a couple from Ecuador who had textile mills for cotton for which Karl was specialized. They offered Karl a job in one of their mills and Karl accepted it. Kurt continued the trip to Bolivia. Their thoughts were, as I was told, that there was a job with a secure income, although it was in a very small place. They did not know what a small place in South America looked like. They compared it with a little village in Europe. As La Paz had only one cotton mill, there was no guarantee that Karl would have a job waiting for him.

The small town was called Atuntaqui, located close to the Colombian border, and not too far from a bigger place, Otavalo. Otavalo is home to the largest indigenous market in South America and is a popular tourist destination today. Life there was very primitive and after a short time Karl got very sick. He had not been informed that a newcomer should not drink water that was not boiled, eat only fruits that you could peel, and to avoid salads. In this area was a convent where he sought help, hoping the nuns could cure him. As he often told me, the nuns took good care of him—they gave him decent food, but did not cure him. It cost him a lot of money, which he did not have, so after awhile he left the convent.

Karl had been able to get an entry visa to Ecuador for his mother, and she was supposed to arrive in Guayaquil in August 1939. By that time Karl decided that he could not bring his mother to this little village, and he would have to move to Quito and find a job. In order to pick up his mother he had to be well. He was told about a curandero—a local healer—and got in contact with him. Through an intermediary, he gave Karl some liquid, which Karl drank and he felt better. But from this time on, he always had trouble with the stomach. A physician in La Paz said it had become chronic—it was some kind of tropical infection—and probably with today's antibiotics it could have been cured. The physician in La Paz tried to cure Karl with a very strict diet, but he always had to be very careful what he ate.

Karl brought also another souvenir from Atuntaqui, a shrunken human head. I never knew the details about how he acquired it, but I am sure he never paid much for it, as he was very short of money. It may have been a gift from a laborer in the factory as appreciation for some help Karl gave to him. In any event, he had this human head. About seventy years ago there were still big stretches of undiscovered jungles and native tribes in South America. According to legend, headhunters were still living in these areas. Anyway, he brought this head to Bolivia. I never saw it and I never wanted to see it or have it in my home. The head, according to description, was the size of a grapefruit, and while Karl lived in Ecuador in some little places shrunken monkey heads were sold as souvenirs. Finally, Karl found a collector of Indian artifacts and guns in La Paz and he traded the head for an antique gun, which I still have. The gun is supposed to be either from the French Revolution or the American Revolution. Although I have no interest in any kind of gun, I still prefer it to a human head.

Karl settled with his mother in Quito and started a small factory making carpets. In the meantime, in La Paz, Kurt wanted to bring his fiancée, Mathilde (Mathi) Popper from England to La Paz and get married. However, the only way he would be able to get a visa for her would be if they were married, so they were married by proxy—Mathi, in the Bolivian Consulate in London; and Kurt, in some government office in La Paz. With those pro-forma certificates, Mathi could come to Bolivia. You would think, like in the movies, a good ending followed. There was only one problem, when Mathi arrived in La Paz, Kurt was sick with typhoid fever. Finally, exactly one year after their proxy marriage, on July 4, 1940, they got married again.

As Kurt still had connections with the textile industry in Europe, he was able to become a representative for different companies, as an agent for textile dyes, yarns and other raw materials. At first he arranged imports from Europe, later from the United States, and through his import work he got to know the owners of the mills in Bolivia. In this capacity, he was able to secure a job for Karl in La Paz and also a visa for their mother, which had been denied earlier. The factory where Karl had worked in Quito was very hard work for him and I don't believe he saw too much future there. He definitely wanted to be together with his family again, so during September 1941 they finally moved to La Paz. A big incentive to move to La Paz was that Mathi was expecting a baby. Unfortunately, that baby died due to negligence at the hospital. In February 1943 their son Ernesto was born. Ernesto moved to the United States in the 1970s from England where he had traveled to train for a career with Mercedes Benz. He and his wife Beatrice have lived in the Los Angeles area for the past thirty years.

SOCIAL LIFE
IN WARTIME LA PAZ

Without a telephone, life was actually less formal. If you wanted to see somebody, you tried to find the home address, which in La Paz, was not difficult. La Paz during the 1940s was a relatively small town. The population of refugees was pretty close knit, so if you were looking for someone, you just had to ask around and someone would know where where to find them. As I mentioned earlier, you were then able to go to their home, simply knock on the door very informally, and usually you were welcome.

After meeting Karl, I very soon fell in love with him. I believe it was both ways. He worked at that time for Seanz & Hijos, which was a textile mill. It was a complete factory, meaning that they produced cloth from the original cotton fiber to the finished material, spinning, weaving and dying—the whole process in the manufacture of cloth. When I met Karl, he worked in the weaving department and was second in charge. His boss was from Switzerland. As I always felt sorry that I was unable to finish my education in the textile school, I was very interested in what he told me about his work and I think he was also happy that I was not completely ignorant about what he was talking about. Not only was I interested in his kind of work; we had common interests in many things. As I was taking English lessons from a German emigrant, I found out that he took lessons from the same teacher. Later when we were married we continued those lessons together for a while.

I often socialized with the girls I worked with at Jenny's. We were more or less the same age and most did not finish their schooling either, but most of them did not miss it and were glad that they could learn a profession, which they always could use. Our thoughts at that time were that it was important to have a profession that you could use all over the world without knowing the language. Many people in La Paz considered that once the situation in the world became peaceful again they would not remain in Bolivia.

When I met Karl's friends, they were a completely different group from the ones I usually socialized with. They were a few years older, had finished their schooling in Austria and had mostly white-collar jobs working in offices. Although grateful to be able to live in La Paz, we commiserated about living in such an isolated country where we were unable to get information about new developments in art, music, science, and new authors, etc. The only information we were able to get was via shortwave radio and as we were not too fluent in English, we depended on the BBC from London with the news in German. This was mostly political, although very important for us; sometimes we received news from Argentina. Even the movies we had in La Paz were not always the latest ones, but I have to say we enjoyed very much going to the movies.

We also tried to keep up with what we had learned in Europe, mainly not to forget it. We tried to solve algebra problems and we tried to figure out how to solve square roots. At that time there were no calculators available and of course no computers yet.

There was one young man in our group, whose name I have forgotten, but who spent a few years working at a tin mine. He had quite a big collection of different minerals he found in the mineshafts. His biggest prize was an imprint of a shell. We had some interesting discussions about how some seashells could be found at an altitude over 13,000 feet. Not having books available for research, we assumed a lot of different theories. I only know that he left for the United States with his collection and sometimes I wonder what happened to him.

But we were not always serious. Being young, we went dancing, to the movies, and naturally to the Austrian Club, where people often met and the events in Europe were always discussed.

Although living far away from the war we were very concerned about the outcome; even in our wildest dreams we could not imagine what really went on in Germany with regard to the concentration camps (in German Konzentrationslager). One of our group, originally from Czechoslovakia, decided to join the Czech freedom fighters. He was an only son and I can imagine how his parents felt when he went to England. He was working at that time in an office of a British company and they promised him that when he returned, he would get his job back, plus a promotion. He did return from the war, married, and changed his name from Schwartz to Shaw.

We did not pay too much attention to the war in the Pacific, as it seemed far away, and unfamiliar to us. We knew about Shanghai because this was one of the few places people could go without an entry visa when leaving Germany. Naturally we knew about

Japan, if not for anything else, but for cheap toys and other merchandise—how this has changed. But with regard to the battles on the different islands and even in the Philippines, these were mostly storybook countries. By the time the atomic bomb fell over Japan, just a year later, we were better informed, as we had obtained maps of the Pacific and could better follow what was happening.

When the United States was attacked by Japan and declared war on Japan and on Germany, Bolivia did too. The German Embassy was closed. There was talk that many Germans in Bolivia belonged to the Fifth Column—a well-known German spy agency. Due to this fact, as long as ships were available, German families, especially the employees from the embassy, were deported back to Germany and later when there was no transportation available to Europe or Germany, the men were sent to Texas. I wish the Japanese or the Germans treated their prisoners as those Germans were treated in Texas. After the war when those internees returned from the U.S.A. they told about the life they had in Texas. Some even had elective surgeries, which at that time were not available in Bolivia. Before the war, there were some big businesses owned by Germans in La Paz. The owners of department stores and their families were the first to be sent back to Germany. When they returned after the war, they did not tell happy stories about their life in Germany, but as much as I know, all of them got their businesses back without any problems.

For us, life was actually not very different than before America entered the war. I remember very well when I heard first of the attack on Pearl Harbor.

It was a Sunday evening and there was a charity Chanukah party to collect money to be used to buy blankets to be sent to Russia for the people in Stalingrad. Before I went with my parents to the party, we heard the sirens and knew right away that something very important was happening. We were very happy to hear that America had entered the fighting, hoping that the war in Europe would soon be over. Of course, we were too optimistic.

We did not have any kind of rationing, but merchandise from the United States was becoming very scarce. We were unable to get stockings, but many other things were replaced with merchandise from Argentina, such as things made of wool, like sweaters. With regard to food, we depended very much on Argentina. Twice a week a train arrived from Buenos Aires that brought butter, meat and many food staples. As we did not have a refrigerator, we had to buy everything fresh. Very often during the rainy season, the train service was interrupted and the first thing we missed was butter. Other staples, like sugar, flour and rice were sometimes only available on the black market and my mother always tried to have some of those staples in reserve.

Vegetables and fruits were mostly produced in Bolivia, partly in the areas of lower altitude. The Altiplano, which surrounded La Paz, had very little agriculture. The only crop which was plentiful was potatoes and of so many different varieties as I have never seen anywhere else. We ate many different kinds, but some looked very suspicious and we never found out how to prepare them. Even later when we were able to afford to eat in a restaurant, we went only to those with European menus, so I was never exposed to those strange-looking potatoes. Some kind of grain was also harvested on the Altiplano, but here too it was some kind I was not familiar with.

While I was living in La Paz, there were no stores where you could buy ready-made dresses. There were special stores that had quite a selection of materials for dresses, suits, etc.; and there were some very good dressmakers, mainly refugees, who made the dresses according catalogues from the United States or Argentina.

VACATIONS IN CHULUMANI

Because living in high altitudes was not considered healthy for Europeans, my parents tried to get away to someplace with a lower altitude each year. However, sometimes when one returned to La Paz it took time to get used to the high altitude again.

In 1944, my parents did not want to return to Cochabamba, given the long train ride. In later years, we flew there. But there were no planes during the war, and even if planes were available, I don't think we would have been able to afford them. My parents wanted to see something different so they decided to go Chulumani in the Yungas Valley. The Yungas Valley is semi-tropical. It's situated between the highlands of the Altiplano and the lowland that borders Brazil and the Amazon basin. The altitude of the village of Chulumani is about 6,000 feet.

My parents decided I should go with them. I invited a friend of mine with whom I worked at Jenny's, Trude Weiss. Trude recently had lost her mother to cancer and she was very happy to join us.

The road to Chulumani was considered (and still is) one of the most dangerous roads in the world. We did not know that yet, so we were not worried. There was a saying that the driver had to be drunk or high on coca to be able to drive this road. The road was mostly one way. In some places, it was a little wider so that a car coming from the other direction could pass. Usually the road was used in the morning one way and the other way in the afternoon. We left early in the morning in a station wagon that belonged

94

to the hotel. We first crossed over the mountains, which were more than 13,000 feet and above tree level. It was very cold. A few hours later, the road went down to about 3,000 feet, and the landscape was full of lush greenery and tropical and warm. We crossed a river, went up some mountains, and arrived at the hotel about lunchtime. The hotel was very pleasant. It wasn't a big hotel, more a family affair, very comfortable, with very good food. It belonged to some Europeans and I believe they had also some interest in agriculture. They had a swimming pool and I loved to swim there, especially since there were no swimming pools in La Paz because of the cold nights.

Coca field

Chulumani was a little village, surrounded by steep mountains. I saw banana trees for the first time there as well as freshly-picked red berries from coffee bushes and I admired the papaya trees with their long, thin trunks and their heavy fruits hanging far up. The main crop of the Yungas was, and I believe still is, coca. Coca is planted on hills on terraces. I don't know if it is done this way to retain water or to provide shade for the little bushes. Indian women pick the leaves of the bushes—similar to the way tea leaves are picked, only tea bushes are taller—and collect the leaves in white aprons and then lay them out on patios to dry. The leaves look similar to bay leaves. The dry leaves are then packed in burlaps bags and sold on the market in La Paz, usually in the same stands that sold potatoes.

Coca leaves were widely used in the local population, mainly by the lower income group. I was told that coca reduced hunger pains and also other kinds of pain and that it could keep you awake. The factory where Karl worked operated twenty-four hours a day, and during Easter week and Carnival week, workers often took extra holidays. Some of the workers who were there were able to work continued shifts without any problem, thanks to the coca leaves. Tea made of coca leaves helped with digestion problems, but you had to be careful not to take too much. Part of the Yungas Valley also supplied the cities of the Altiplano with bananas, vegetables and other fruits. The area around Cochabamba was more temperate and vegetables that we were used to in Europe were cultivated there.

Before I went to Chulumani, I needed a root canal and I was told there was a good dentist living there. At that time for the treatment of root canal you to had to go to the dentist a few times to clean out the tooth, or root. I went to the dentist, who didn't have electricity. His dental motor was with a foot pedal and the floor of his office was a dirt floor. The room did not have a window. The open door gave enough light so he could see what he was doing. Before I opened my mouth, I requested that he wash his hands. Luckily, he had running water. But somehow he did what he was supposed to do and no harm was done to my tooth. The hotel had a generator, so thankfully we had electricity there.

My parents had planned to stay in Chulumani for two weeks. After being there for one week, to my great surprise, Karl came. He also had vacation time due and wanted to spend the time with us. There, on the 16th of August, he asked me to marry him. My parents were very happy to have Karl as a son-in-law and later, when my father got to know Karl better, he became very fond of him. My father was always busy improving his work with new methods and as Karl was also mechanically inclined, my father had someone with whom he could discuss his inventions.

As I was in the second week of my vacation with my parents, and Karl arrived one week into our vacation for his two-week holiday, we spent just one week together. Karl asked me to take his brother a jar of marmalade as his way of introducing myself to the Mautner family. He gave me the address where his brother lived and I did not find it unusual in any way just to show up. Apparently Karl had mentioned to his family why he was spending his vacations in Chulumani, so they were not surprised when I arrived at their door. On the contrary, they were very pleased to see me. When Kurt Mautner opened the door for me,

I immediately recognized him and his wife as the couple I had met when I was in Cochabamba. This was the couple who had spent all the time by themselves and never joined the other guests in the boarding house when everybody went to the city. It was quite a surprise for both of us to meet again. To show how pleased they were to meet me, they introduced me to the youngest member of the family and showed me their son Ernesto. He was half asleep. It seems as if it were just yesterday—he opened his big blue eyes and looked at me. When I came home I told my mother that I just seen the most beautiful baby.

When Karl returned from Chulumani, he introduced me to his mother, who was very happy to meet me and welcomed me into the Mautner family. Everyone approved of our choice. There was only one thing that Karl asked me— if we could live with his mother. Karl's mother had circulatory problems, which made living in the altitude worse. I am sure that today with the advance of the medical profession and research it could have been easy to take care of. I answered, as I was living with my parents, that I would be able to live with his mother, too.

GETTING MARRIED

Shortly after we returned from Chulumani, my sister Lilly and her husband, Ernst, found out that one could get a visiting or tourist visa to Chile. As most people did not consider Bolivia a permanent home, Lilly and Ernst decided to go to Chile with the thought that once they were established there, we would all follow. My boss Jenny and her family also went to Chile. Consequently, I lost my job, but I did not look for another one, as I had plans to get married and Karl's salary was enough that we would not depend on any income I would be able to make.

There was only one problem with this visa. It was a tourist visa and everybody thought that once in Chile there would be no problem to get a permit for permanent residence. Unfortunately, it was not possible and Ernst definitely did not wanted to live in a place illegally, where he could be deported. Jenny and her family returned also after six months and again opened a store. By this time, I was not interested in working for her.

There were several reasons why I did not return to work for Jenny. First, I was getting married and Karl thought I should learn to cook from my mother, who was a very good cook. In this respect my mother was not such a motivated teacher. I remember her saying: "If you want to cook, you might not be able to make gourmet meals, but you won't starve. If you want to learn to cook, there are cookbooks which can be a big help." Unfortunately, there were no cookbooks available in La Paz; the only ones we had were books we had brought from Austria. Because the preparation of food in the altitude was so different from the way you cooked in Europe, those cookbooks were not so helpful. The fruits and vegetables in the market were new to us, and we had to get used to their taste and also how to prepare them in order to like them.

Another reason for not returning to work for Jenny was there was a new ordinance in La Paz that you had to remove your hat in the movie theaters so that the person who sat behind you did not have their view disturbed. People often bought special clothing and hats to go to the theater, but the new ordinance cut down the demand for hats.

Casa Elite
Lilly's dress shop, La Paz

I was glad that my sister and her husband returned from Chile, as I would have missed her very much at my wedding. After they returned, they finally rented an apartment. Before they left, they had only one rented room and my mother always cooked for the whole family. My parents helped them to buy a business. It was a well-established store and the owner was selling it because she was leaving Bolivia. The location of the store was on a main street, leading to the suburbs. It was a specialty shop for women and partly carried imported merchandise, mainly from Argentina. Later when the war was over, merchandise became available again from the United States.

Karl's boss in the factory was from Switzerland and his contract was due to expire in August 1945. He did not intend to renew it, as he wanted to return home with his family and Karl was to take over the weaving department. We decided to get married on June 3rd, so that Karl could easily take time off from his work, while there was still somebody in charge of the department. When we set our wedding day, we were hoping to get married in peacetime. When Germany surrendered on May 7th, the war in the Pacific was still on. We were sure that it would be over very soon too.

The factory where Karl worked was on the outskirts of La Paz in an industrial section. The company had its own station wagon and supplied transportation for its white-collar employees. Karl and his mother shared an apartment with another couple, so we had to look for an apartment for the three of us. At that time it was important for Karl that we have an apartment where it was easy to get to the factory. The factory was working twenty-four hours a day, and it was expected that Karl sometimes show up at the factory during the night shift. So, often when we returned in the evening from the movies or some other outings, Karl took a taxi, to see what was going on during the night shift.

Usually that taxi waited until he did his inspection and then he returned home.

We were lucky and found a nice apartment that was well located for our needs, and now we were busy furnishing it and getting things ready for our wedding. In Bolivia, it was not the way it was in the United States, where you go to a department store and just select what you would like to have, make a bridal list and hope friends will help you. First, there was no department store where you could order. It was still wartime and many things were not available. One had to order everything specially made for you, including linens. For furnishings, you definitely had to order everything from a carpenter who made the things according to your drawings or from catalogues. There were a lot of refugees in La Paz like us. One was an excellent carpenter from Czechoslovakia. He had built some furniture for my parents with which they were very satisfied, and whatever he made for us came out perfectly—just as we wanted it.

Although it was a very happy time for me, it was very much dampened by the news we got from Europe. As my parents found out, none of their brothers or sisters survived the war. Later we discovered that most of my cousins survived and were living in all parts of the world.

After we were married, we often remarked about all the difficulties we had before our wedding and our honeymoon until we really could settle down as a couple. According to superstition of my parents, it was considered bad luck if one of your close families made your wedding dress or the rings. So my father gave gold for the making of our rings to a Bolivian, who disappeared with the gold. We then found somebody else to make our rings. The photographer we had hired to take our photos broke his arm and we could not get a replacement at that time. Although Karl as well as Kurt had cameras, we never thought that anyone of our friends or the family would take any photos, so we have no pictures from our wedding. The wedding was very nice; we had a catered reception for our family and friends in our new apartment and everybody had a good time. After we returned from our honeymoon, we took a day to dress again in our wedding outfits and had some wedding photos taken.

Besides beautiful vicuña fur bedcovers, Kurt and Mathi gave us as a special wedding present of tickets to fly to Cochabamba for our honeymoon. For both of us this was to be our first flight. For Sunday night Karl made reservations in a hotel and according to the plan we were supposed to leave on Monday. When we arrived at the hotel we found out that through a mistake they did not have a room for us. La Paz was not so big as to have many alternative hotels. The manager realized that he had made a mistake and gave us a room. The next morning when we got up, we found a note at our door saying, "This room is occupied by a honeymoon couple" and that this person should sleep in the office of the hotel.

The airport for La Paz, El Alto Airport, was located on the Altiplano. It was one of the highest airports in the world—at 13,323 feet. At that time, only small planes could be used to fly over the high Andes. The plane we were supposed to take came from Lima, Peru, continued to Cochabamba and then further to Brazil. It was considered one of the most

On our honeymoon, Cochabamba, 1945

difficult routes and was only made when the weather
conditions were perfect; flights were not scheduled
daily.

   Before we left for the airport we found out that
the flight was delayed and we would probably leave the
following day. The next day, Tuesday, when we arrived
at the airport, we were told that some military personnel were on the plane (the war in the Pacific was still
being fought) and military personnel had preference.
As a result, we were told there would not be room for
us on the flight. At that time you were still able to talk
to the captain, especially in an airport as small as the

one in La Paz. In our best English, which was not very good, we tried to explain to the captain that we were on our honeymoon and just had to leave. The captain was very cooperative, and made every effort to find a way for us to fly that day, by calculating the weight the plane already carried and adding ours (we were both very skinny then) to see if it would be possible. At first he decided he could take us without our luggage. He then reconsidered, and offered to take our suitcases as his private luggage. So thanks to the courtesy of the pilot we made it to Cochabamba. When we arrived in Cochabamba he gave me a kiss, to the surprise of the other passengers, and wished us good luck.

Once in Cochabamba, we stayed at a very nice new hotel, which had a swimming pool and tennis courts, which at the time was very unusual in Bolivia. Although we did not have much money, Karl was of the opinion, "We are only once in your life on a honeymoon, let's not pinch pennies—we can save later and have the best memories to last a lifetime." On our return flight we had no further problems, but it was a very bumpy flight. The hand luggage fell from the luggage rack, and the steward was just as sick as I was.

STARTING OUR MARRIED LIFE

When we returned from our honeymoon, we settled down in our new apartment and got used to our new life. With the help of my parents, we had it nicely furnished and Kurt did his part for his mother.

Our apartment had a bathroom, but of course there was no shower, as hot water heaters were very unusual in apartments or houses at that time. Kurt later moved to a house where there was a water heater and they probably had a shower there. To heat the water for a bath, you filled the tub with water and put in a contraption called a submersible, which was 220 volts. When you saw the water steaming, which took about one hour, you were about ready to take the bath. You could not put your hand in because with the 220 volts you could get electrocuted. You took out the submersible, and added some cold water to have the proper temperature. We usually did this in the evening, but very often the water was turned off during the evening hours, so we had to open the window to cool the water. When the water was finally the right temperature the room was very cold and we had to put an electric heater into the room to heat the room. The nights were usually very cold. As you can imagine, taking a simple bath was a big undertaking. We always had some big pots filled with water for other uses, as we never knew when the water would be cut off.

In order to be useful, Karl's mother wanted to do the cooking. Since I did not know how to cook, I did not mind. We also had a maid who did all the cleaning and washing. It would not have been right that I should do this work. Once when my mother-in-law went on vacation, she prepared for me a little cookbook with easy recipes, as she was afraid we would starve. Unfortunately, I misplaced or lost this little cookbook. It would be interesting to see what was easy to prepare in La Paz, considering that beef had to be cooked in this altitude for four or five hours to be edible.

I was never able to finish school and, as mentioned before, making hats was going out of style. Working with felt, my hands were always dirty as you hardly ever could get the dark felt out from under your fingernails. I think it was Kurt's idea that I should take a course and learn typing and to find an American to teach me English. As I still knew shorthand from my school in Vienna, I decided I could adjust it to English and for Spanish I bought a book and learned from it. It was more or less a thought to keep me busy. It was very fortunate that I took those lessons and later when I was in Caracas it was really a lifesaver for me, because as a bilingual secretary I was able to support my first son, Willy and myself.

I found an American missionary to teach me English. She was from the Baha'i faith and spoke very little Spanish, so we had to converse exclusively in English. Being a missionary, she explained to me everything about her religion, which I found very interesting. Later I found out she married a Christian and said goodbye to being a missionary. Kurt lent me his small typewriter so I could practice. After I finished my typing course, my English was getting better. By that time, I had also finished the book with the instructions for Spanish shorthand. I started looking for a job and I found one really to my liking. It was very close to where we lived in a big Bolivian company, "Saenz y Hijos." They had a glass factory, a lumber-yard and a department for import.

My job was in the department for import and representation. My boss was also an emigrant from Germany. He was the best boss you can imagine. Each department had its own secretary and we did not overwork ourselves. Every morning my boss gave me the newspapers to read, while he checked the mail. When he was finished with the mail, he usually allowed me to finish the papers while he went to talk with other department heads, including the representative from Socony Oil (which merged later with Exxon Mobil.) I also took care of the secretarial work for this representative, but he did not have much work for me. In general, I did not feel overworked.

As none of the secretaries were very busy, some brought to the office wool and spent time knitting very nice things, which were very useful in the cold climate of La Paz. However, I did not feel comfortable knit-ting at the office, so I read magazines in my free time. It was 1946 and the first merchandise from the United States was becoming available. Saenz y Hijos obtained export permits from the United States and was able, among other things, to import refrigerators and cars. The imported refrigerators worked very well and everyone who obtained one was very satisfied. The six cars (made by Nash) that were imported arrived in good condition, nice and shiny, but they were not equipped to work in the altitude of La Paz with those hilly streets. I assume they needed some special adjust-ment, so finally those cars ended up in Cochabamba, which is at a much lower altitude and has no hills.

During the early 1940s the presence of oil and gas was discovered in the south of Bolivia toward the border of Paraguay. While I was working for Socony, the company started to explore it further and started to bring the first machinery into this region. Parts of the equipment were very long pipes, which had to be transported through some very small villages or towns. Sometimes those trucks had to go around corners and the houses were too close for the lengths of the pipes. This was a major problem. I never found out if the company built roads bypassing those little towns or whether it might have been cheaper to demolish those houses and rebuild new ones later on.

We got married in June and during the same month two of our friends married too. One was Heinz Frankenstein, Karl's best friend. He was together with Karl when we met at the dance. He married a girl from Cochabamba. The other one was Heinz Landesman. He was originally from Czechoslovakia. He married a girl who came from Belgium. During the war she fled with her parents through France over the Pyrenees into Spain and finally landed in Bolivia. We met occasionally in our apartments. I will never forget our visit to the Landesmans' apartment. They served us ice cream, although I don't know how they kept it cold, as they did not have a refrigerator. Their apartment had a fireplace, though, and they wanted to show us how sophisticated they were by lighting a fire in the fireplace. It drizzled that night and due to the combination of the altitude and the light rain, a lot of smoke was produced, which went back into the room. As I was the only non-smoker, I was especially sensitive to smoke. When we returned home I fainted. Apparently, I had carbon monoxide poisoning. We were a little bit scared, but the next day I felt fine again, so I didn't even go to the doctor to be checked.

TAKING ADVANTAGE OF HOLIDAYS

Bolivia had a lot of holidays and the factory was closed for a few days during Carnival from Sunday until Thursday. Many workers did not show up the whole week. The same was true for Easter and there were also about three days off during the national holiday in August. Besides these, there were other different religious and national paid holidays.

Hotel Tiquina, 1946

We tried to take advantage of those short holidays to leave town. A few times we went to Tiquina on Lake Titicaca, which was about four or five hours from La Paz. Lake Titicaca is the highest navigable lake of the world at 12,507 feet. Tiquina is located on the narrowest part of the lake. To get to Tiquina, your car was loaded on a boat and brought across the lake. The whole procedure was very primitive and you crossed the lake on a separate boat.

Market in Tiquina

The hotel itself was located on a bluff with a beautiful view of the blue lake and in the background you could see some peaks of the snow-covered Andes. The hotel had its own electric generator and at bedtime they turned the generator off and we had only candlelight. I don't know why the hotel did not supply the guests with flashlights. I can only assume that during that time batteries for flashlights were in short supply or were very expensive. There were beautiful hikes around the lake, which we enjoyed very much and as my father loved to hike, sometimes my parents joined us.

Once, during Carnival, we went together with the Landesmans to Copacabana, which is also located on Lake Titicaca. Copacabana is considered a special religious place, because of the Virgin of Copacabana. To get to Copacabana you have to pass Tiquina and then it still takes you a few hours to arrive at the town.

Copacabana is very close to the border of Peru and we made an excursion once to Puno to see what it was like. We unfortunately spent too little time there to get any impression of the town. The center of Copacabana is dominated by the church. Behind the church is a hill that has some sacred meaning. In the afternoon we walked up some steps up the hill while the sun was setting. The white church looked like a Moorish temple to me and because of the sunset was all in pink.

Lake Titicaca

The most interesting part of our trip was when we went on a boat to the southern part of the lake to visit "Isla del Sol"—the sun island. According to legend, the God of the Incas lived there. When we stepped off the boat onto the little island, we found a little creek coming down from the hills, surrounded by trees and the floor covered with forget-me-not blue flowers. It was the most amazing sight! It looked like paradise to me. I found there some rose quartz and I still have it.

Escaderia in Isla del Sol, 1946

Rebuilt Escaderia in Isla del Sol, 1946

There were over eighty ruins on the island, including an "escadaria" or stairway originally built by the Incas. It was later restored. To this day, there are no paved roads or cars allowed on the island.

As we were in Copacabana during Carnival, naturally there were parties going on, with the people dressed in beautiful and colorful native clothing and dancing in the streets and squares to typical Bolivian music. Suddenly some of the dancers recognized Karl, their boss from the factory, and invited me to join them in the dance. The melodies were actually very simple and slow and the dancing also slow as in that altitude even the natives were unable to do things too fast. However, with the influence of coca leaves or alcohol they were able to dance for twenty-four hours or more.

To the delight of the workers I accepted their invitation. If I had rejected them it would have been a big offense. The Indian population was sometimes very moody, especially when they were high on Pisco (a national alcoholic drink) or beer. You had to be on friendly terms with your workers to get something accomplished.

Carnival, in general, was a very big celebration in Bolivia, but definitely it cannot be compared with the one in Rio de Janeiro. On Sunday morning, the Bolivian Society brought their children in beautiful costumes for a parade on one of the main streets. It was beautiful to look at those children. The other population danced for three days up and down the different streets, each group with their own musical instruments. Naturally after so much celebration, not too many workers showed up on Wednesday for work. This was a problem if so many workers were missing, but people who chewed coca leaves were able to work some consecutive shifts and in this way Karl was able to have uninterrupted production.

Children's carnival in La Paz, 1939

Street musicians in La Paz

Karl had a few very knowledgeable mechanics working for him. One day he found out that one of his mechanics was losing his eyesight. After getting a report from an ophthalmologist saying that he was not able to help this man, the worker asked for a leave of absence to be able to go to his village and to see a curandero or healer. After a few weeks he returned as a healthy man and as long as we were living in La Paz, the mechanic never had any more problems with his eyes. After a while Karl noticed that another worker had eye trouble and so he asked the first one to give him or the worker the name of the village so that he could be healed too. To his surprise, he refused to give Karl the name of the village and we never found out why this was such a big secret.

Factory football team

Karl really respected his workers and he had an excellent rapport with them. One time, he sponsored a football team for them, and we paid for the uniforms and the refreshments afterwards out of our own pocket.

Karl at the factory with mechanics

CHANGES IN MY FAMILY

Not long after we were married, my parents found a very nice apartment in a residential area. It was close to the apartment where Lilly lived and also close to their business. It was the upper floor of a nice house. My father could use one room for his work and there was a little room to receive customers. Besides these, there was a living room, a dining room and a beautiful view from the bedroom. The bedroom over-looked a lovely garden, which had a very big tree, something that was very unusual in La Paz.

My father, David Weingrün, at work

The apartment was across from the Argentine Embassy, which was actually very pleasant. There was one drawback to this. At that time, Bolivia often had a change of government and the deposed president and people from his government went for asylum to embassies until it was safe for them to leave the country. While the president or people from his administration were staying at the embassy for security, the embassy was surrounded by the military. At night, the soldiers liked to shoot into the air, perhaps just to disturb the inhabitants of their sleep. I'm not sure why they did this. Fortunately, my parents' bedroom was in the back of the house so it did not bother them much. On the contrary, they felt well protected.

Those revolutions or changes of government were usually very peaceful. In the morning you heard there was going to be a different president. In spite of the change of government and different disturbances, the markets and grocery stores were usually open during the morning hours, so you could do your shopping. We tried to keep enough food at home so that we didn't need to go out unless it was necessary. Offices were usually closed for a few days, so it was like some kind of vacation, although during the afternoon and definitely evening and night, everyone stayed home.

In all the years I was living in La Paz there was one revolution that was really scary. It lasted a few days and a lot of shooting was going on. But the markets were still open in the morning hours. I was already married when this uprising happened. We lived at that time very close to the armory. The revolutionaries stormed the armory and took hold of the rifles. Luckily the ammunition depot was out of town, in a secure location. From our window we could see the Indians walking with the stolen rifles and examining the rifles to figure out how they worked. Since we did not know that the armory had no ammunition, we were a little scared and stayed in a room that did not have a window toward the street.

As mentioned, usually when there were those changes in government, the president left peacefully and got asylum in an embassy until it was safe for him and his family to leave the country. One president refused to leave and was finally killed and his body was hanged on a lantern post in front of the parliament. Those changes of government were not too frequent and in general it was peaceful living in Bolivia, more so I suspect than what was going on in Europe.

On October 14, 1946, our family increased as Lilly gave birth to a healthy baby boy whom they named, Alfred Zenon (Zenon was the name of my mother's youngest brother, who perished during the Holocaust.) It was my parents' first grandchild and they were very happy. I, too, was very proud to have a new nephew. Very often on Sunday afternoon we went to visit Lilly and Ernst and watch Freddie, as we called him, get his bath. After bathing time we usually left, because Freddie was a very poor eater—at least when Lilly tried to feed him—so it was no fun to watch that. Lilly had at that time a very good maid who loved the baby. When Lilly was working in the store, the maid took care of the baby and I believe that she had no problems feed-ing the baby, because he developed very nicely. So it was no problem for Lilly to continue working, as she had a very reliable person to take care of the house and the baby. Besides the store was very close to their home and she always could go home and take care of whatever was necessary. I am sure that my mother, who also lived very close by, visited her grandchild and made sure that everything was all right.

MY LIFE CHANGES,
I BECOME A HOMEMAKER

Karl always tried to get some connections with factories in other South American countries to get some jobs elsewhere. We did not see much future in living permanently in La Paz. This was partly because of the altitude and it also might have been that the grass was greener on the other side of the border. Bolivia was and still is very rich in minerals, but it was and still is a very poor country, perhaps because it does not have access to the ocean. The lower altitudes were mostly tropical and had very poor roads to bring produce to the population in the cities. While I was living there, much of our food was imported, mostly from Argentina and some from Chile. With both countries, there were rail connections. There was only one problem. During the rainy season, the rail connections were often interrupted and we were not able to get some food staples. For this reason we always tried to have for instance, rice, sugar and flour in reserve. We could not buy butter in advance and sometimes we just had to manage without it.

Despite the challenges of our daily life, I will be forever being thankful that Bolivia accepted us when we needed a place to escape from Hitler and that we could live there peacefully and support ourselves with decent work.

Although we hoped to leave Bolivia for a more hospitable climate before having a baby, by the time we were married for about two years we did not see that we would be able to leave Bolivia in the near future. So we decided to start a family. I enjoyed my job, but Karl's income was enough that I did not have to work. Whatever money I made we were able to save.

We decided the best way to start a family was to be on vacation, so we went again to Cochabamba. We traveled to where we had spent our honeymoon, and this time we had no problem with our flights. A few months later our physician confirmed that I was expecting a baby.

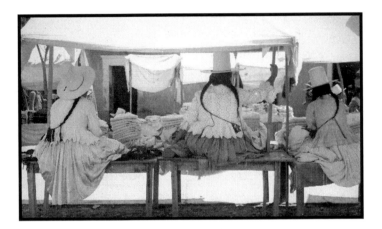

Market in Cochabamba

When I was in my third month of pregnancy, Karl's mother suddenly passed away. It was not totally unexpected, as she was a sick woman, having frequent problems with her blood circulation, which weakened her heart. This was the reason why she could not live by herself. I am quite sure with today's medications and not living at that altitude, things would have been different. However, despite her health challenges she felt useful up to the last day of her life. She enjoyed her one grandson and was looking forward to another grandchild.

I don't know why my parents did not want us to stay in the apartment where my mother–in–law passed away. Their reason was that it might affect my pregnancy. At the time my parents had a big apartment, so we were able move in with our beds and other essentials and occupy their living room. As soon as we were settled, we started to look for an apartment close to the home of my parents. Karl's brother and my sister lived also in this area. We wanted be close to the entire family. I think after about two months, we found a duplex in a new building about three blocks away from my parents. The owner lived on the first floor and we on the second. The only disadvantage was that there was a very steep hill to climb between our houses.

But we had beautiful views of all La Paz and especially of Mt. Illimani, which is one of the most beautiful mountains I have ever seen. As the altitude of Mt. Illimani is more than 21,000 feet, it is always covered by white snow. In the evening at a certain time of the year when the moon rises behind the mountain, it changed color to purple and at sunset it was sometimes red. If I could paint the mountain with all the colors nobody would believe that a mountain could have such beautiful colors.

We enjoyed the beautiful view from our apartment very much. On August 6th, the national holiday, there were always fireworks to celebrate the occasion. In 1948, the city of La Paz celebrated that it was 400 years since it was founded. There was a very spectacular firework show, which, together with my parents, we enjoyed very much as we had a special view from our windows. Bolivia had many occasions for fireworks, but this was so outstanding that I still remember it.

Mt. Illimani

By that time Karl was boss of the weaving department and he could call for the station wagon from the company pick him up wherever we lived. Naturally it had to be in a reasonable distance.

It was the beginning of a very happy time for me. I had so much to learn, besides being pregnant. I never needed to know how to cook or keep house because Karl's mother took care of everything. Now I was on my own. The servant we had when we were all living together got married and left. I had to hire another "muchacha," which at that time was not difficult. However, very often after the girls saved a little money, they went back to their villages.

One problem I had was that sometimes they took things, which was challenging for me. They were often not very valuable things, mostly food staples, which I'm sure they needed, and which I would gladly have given them if they had asked. Canned food was a luxury in La Paz so I kept it locked up, although I doubt that the girls would have dared to take such a valuable item home. Later, when Willy was born, I had a very nice girl and I always gave her food to take home. She was especially appreciative when I gave her old magazines or newspapers. She was actually educated in a convent and did beautiful embroidery. Because of the war just ending, there was still a shortage of merchandise. In La Paz, nobody would throw out a pair of socks—if it had a hole, you would mend it. This girl did a very good job of mending.

During that time our close friends, the Landesmans, left for Buenos Aires and we never heard from them again. Our other friends, the Frankensteins went to New York. Unfortunately, Heinz had an accident in the New York subway (at least that what I was told) and his pregnant wife returned to Cochabamba to be with her family. I never heard from her either. However, we made new friends, as people got to know each other in the neighborhood where we lived. Among our new friends were Andres and Idel Simon. They had a little girl and she was also expecting a baby at that time. We stayed in contact for many years until Andres passed away in 2005 and Idel in 2007.

I shopped nearly every day, since, as I have mentioned, without a refrigerator we worried that food would not stay fresh. I discovered, however, that in the cold nights in La Paz, that I could use the windowsills to keep perishable food fresh. As meat needed to cook for a long time, and we usually had our main meal at noon, very often I cooked enough for two days. The windowsills then became very handy.

On the way to the market

Very close to my parents' home was a market hall, actually like a big farmers market, but covered. Usually when I went to the market I stopped at my mother's house and told her what I wanted to buy and asked her how to prepare it. I couldn't rely on my

German cookbooks. Since we had no car, I walked back and forth to the market. This was not a problem, as at the entrance of the market were boys who were always waiting to help you carry your purchases home for a tip. If one was very generous, one also gave them some food, as those were very poor children.

I enjoyed cooking. Actually the things came out very edible. I didn't have to throw out much because I had ruined it. Another thing that made keeping house easy was that I never had to wash dishes or peel potatoes or other vegetables. I had my help. The owner of the house where we lived had a telephone and Mathi, my sister-in-law, had one too. It was connected with Kurt's office and whenever my "muchacha" did not show up, I called Mathi and she sent me help as she had two. By the time I was keeping house, they lived in a bigger place and their servants stayed overnight.

The stove I used for cooking had two burners— actually it was an improved Primus cooker. For baking, I put a hood over those burners for temperature control. You just opened the door on the front and if it felt warm you put the cake mixture in. Prepared cake mixes were unknown and you had to do everything from scratch. The first time I made a chocolate cake, our friends, the Simons, came over to visit. It was in the evening and I very proudly told Idel that I was baking a cake and opened the door of the so-called oven to show her what I was doing. She corrected me, saying that opening the oven door before the cake is set would not allow the cake to rise. My curiosity won me over. I wanted to see what was going on and it actually did not hurt the cake much. When it was finished, we all enjoyed the still-warm cake. Usually this cake requires a butter frosting, which makes the cake very rich.

In Venezuela, I made this cake frequently. Because it was such a foolproof recipe and everybody liked it very much, I gave the recipe to everyone who asked me for it. The result was that I was often served my own chocolate cake when I was invited to friends' homes. Even when I visited Caracas in the 1970s, my hostess very proudly served me my cake. I stopped baking this cake in California.

OUR FAMILY INCREASES

In La Paz, baby showers were unknown and stores hardly had any merchandise for newborns—you had to do everything by yourself or order it from some dressmaker. On top of it, because of the cold weather and poor heating, one needed lots of warm clothing for the newborn. I was busy knitting baby jackets and blankets and sewing shirts. With regard to diapers, Karl got from the factory a whole roll of cotton material, which I cut and then hemmed for diapers. In La Paz, you used on top of the cotton diapers flannel diapers and this material would have been too heavy to hem. To prevent the borders from unraveling, I embroidered them. So you can see I was very busy getting ready for the arrival of my baby. Also the care I got from my physician was very different from the care you receive in the United States. My doctor never took my weight or my blood pressure. The only thing he required was that I have a monthly urine test. With regard to diet, he informed me to avoid any canned food. As canned food in general was considered a luxury, I never used very much anyway so I did not miss it. Since La Paz did not have fresh milk or products that contained calcium, I received regular calcium injections during my pregnancy. I received no instructions at all for exercise.

In Bolivia we were always very concerned with germs and infections. We washed everything very carefully. We did not have a washing machine, but this was no bother for me as for this I had a girl to do it. But I did worry about the laundry. I could not see to the patio where my "muchacha" hung up the laundry, and I thought some pieces might fall on the dirty floor. So I had her iron everything for disinfection, including the diapers, as I assumed that the heat of the iron killed all the germs. As long as I lived in Bolivia my baby always had ironed diapers.

Our home in La Paz

Willy was born on Friday, February 20, 1948, at 4 a.m. On Thursday afternoon I visited Lilly at the store. My mother always enjoyed very much visiting Lilly and Ernst's store, so she was there too. I had arranged with Karl to pick me up at the store on the way home from the factory. As we had no telephone, my mother thought I should not be home alone at this late stage of my pregnancy, so in the afternoon after my "muchacha" left, I either went to visit my parents or went to Lilly's store and sometimes I went with Lilly to visit Freddie. Lilly had a very good maid and who also slept in the house, but Lilly still went home sometimes during the day to check if everything was all right.

When Karl came to pick me up, I told him that I felt strange and as I was already past my due date, we decided to take a taxi and go right to the hospital. When we arrived there and after the doctor examined me, he told us the baby would probably be born the next day. We asked him if we should go home, but he mentioned that he would stay as he lived very far from the hospital, so we decided to stay, too. That was the right decision. There was a nurse on duty who regularly checked on me and after midnight she said we better hurry to the delivery room. The delivery room was not heated, on doctor's orders, as the baby was not due before the next day. So suddenly everything became a big rush, and in the morning I had a healthy baby boy. Karl always wanted to be present when his child was born, but that was a big no-no at that time in La Paz. However, they did not have time to ask him to leave the delivery room. Here he was with his clothing from the factory, which I am sure had a lot of germs, holding his new son!

In the morning, Karl left to inform the family about our new son and bring me the clothing I had prepared for the baby and myself, as the hospital did not supply us with enough. He also arranged for our private nurse, which was a necessity in La Pa. This nurse also came home with us to help me and teach me how to take care of the baby. The nurse whom I had contracted was actually a friend of Kurt and Mathi Mautner and the mother of Karl's friend Heinz Frankenstein, the same friend who was at the tea dance when I met Karl.

The nurse was very efficient, actually too efficient for my liking. She was a refugee from Germany and before she got married she worked as a nurse. I understood that during World War I she was in the army as a nurse. She wanted everything very exact— the baby had to be fed at a certain time, even if the baby was crying because he was hungry, and not ten minutes earlier or ten minutes later. That, as she explained to me, would a difference of twenty minutes and would be very unhealthy. Somehow Willy and I survived the military drill.

On Sunday the entire family visited the baby and me. It is the Jewish custom to name the baby with a name that begins with at least the first letter of the name of an ancestor. Karl's mother's name was Gertrude and his father's name was Gustav. I wanted to name the baby George and Karl was so happy he agreed to everything. The family did not like the name too much and what started to bother me was that the German nurse could not pronounce the name properly. So after two days we changed the name to Guillermo, but called him Willy. As a middle name we choose Fred, after my favorite cousin who perished in Mauthausen concentration camp during World War II.

As Mathi had visited us already on Saturday and had noticed that the little jacket I had made for Willy was too big for him, she went home and made a new one, washed it (and I don't know how she could dry it), and Willy had a proper fitting jacket and a very proud aunt. Mathi was very handy at knitting; I have never seen anybody knit so fast. She could finish a whole back of a sweater for an adult in one evening.

At that time, you had to stay for about one week in the hospital and you were not allowed to get up before the fifth day. On Saturday, when we came home, the Bris was planned for the following day. We told my nurse (whom we called "The General") that she could go home for the night, because we wanted to celebrate as a family alone. Willy was sound asleep and we decided to go to sleep too. Suddenly we heard a strange noise coming from the bathroom and when Karl opened the door we realized that a water pipe had burst and the bathroom was flooded. So we did not have such a nice peaceful night. The next day everything worked according to our plans. I had the nurse still for a few days and then we were on our own. I tried to nurse my son but somehow it was very painful for me and after a few months I had to give it up.

Preparing a baby's formula in La Paz was a challenge since La Paz did not have fresh milk. I used powdered milk, which came from the United States. It was very time consuming, as you had to sterilize everything. In La Paz, we had to boil the water for the formula for about twenty minutes. It was the same with the bottles and all the utensils I used to prepare. Later, when I started to give Willy solid food, this also involved a lot of work, as in La Paz canned baby food was unknown and I had to prepare everything from scratch. Of course, there were no food processors then. I had to strain everything and I definitely did not let my maid handle the food for the baby.

For a while I had a maid who complained that giving the baby a daily bath was unhealthy because it thinned the skin. I knew of some mothers who also boiled the water for the bath of their babies, because

Willy, age 5 months
with Karl, and with Edith

babies like to put their wet fingers into the mouth and it might contain some germs. "The General" nurse said a little water that was not boiled before would not do any harm; on the contrary, it would build up some resistance to germs.

AN UNEXPECTED CHANGE
AND A BIG MOVE

Although Karl was always interested in leaving La Paz, when we had the baby, we decided to stay for a while. We did not believe to move with a baby was appropriate.

Sometimes you make plans and things turn out differently. Shortly after Willy was born, Kurt, Karl's brother, who represented some big American companies in Bolivia, decided to visit some of those companies. At the same time, Mathi wanted to visit her sister, who lived in the States and whom she had not seen since she left Vienna. As there was finally no more war, one was again able to travel.

When Kurt visited New York, he met the managers of Sudamtex, who were building a new cotton mill in Venezuela and were looking for people with experience in this field. Kurt told them about his brother Karl. Following some correspondence Karl got an offer and contract to work in their factory in Maracay, Venezuela, not too far from their home office in Caracas. We were under the impression in La Paz that Karl had a very high paying salary, not realizing that living expenses in general were cheap in Bolivia and we were going to a country were expenses were high. Personnel hired in the United States to work in Venezuela usually got a thirty-percent living allowance.

We did not know much about Venezuela beyond my visit to La Guaira, which had been our first stop in South America. During this one-day visit we did not pay any attention to the climate or anything else of importance. I only remembered that it was hot and that people looked different from Europeans. One thing that most impressed me was the women smoking cigars.

We were informed that Maracay was about four hours by car from Caracas. In Maracay, the weather was definitely tropical. For us, coming from the cold climate of La Paz, getting used to the tropical heat was to be a difficult adjustment. At that time air conditioning was unknown, at least in Maracay.

After exactly one year we gave up our apartment and were packing our things for our move to Venezuela. The company had agreed to move all of our household things. We were not sure what we would need to set up our household in Maracay. During the war years in Bolivia, and I believe all over the world, you were not able to buy many household articles, like pots and pans. Besides my wedding presents most of what we owned were what Karl's mother had brought from Europe. Those things had already quite a few years of use. Now after the war suddenly there were new and beautiful merchandise in the stores and I did not believe that those things would be available in Venezuela, especially not in the interior where we going to live. So I bought new things and had them shipped to our new destination. Arriving in Venezuela, I found that everything was available and in a much bigger selection.

As nothing ever goes easily, we had some problems getting visas for Venezuela, although I don't know why. Karl had already resigned from his job and we had given up the apartment, so we moved back to my parents' apartment until the time we got our visas.

My parents were actually happy about the delay, as they could be around their grandchild for a longer time.

In La Paz, we had lived a nice apartment and I was happy being a mother and housewife close to my family and having many good friends. Suddenly, there was to be a big change. Although we were looking forward to our new life in Venezuela, this made our leaving a bittersweet time.

FAMILY PHOTOS

Lilly, Ernst
and a young Alfredo "Freddie" Grab
La Paz, 1952

Willy, 5 months
with cousin Ernesto, 5 years, in 1948

David and Rosa Weingreen
New York, 1954

Edith in Cochabamba, 1947

Lilly and Edith, Caracas, 1953

Karl Mautner, Vienna, 1939

Karl Mautner, La Paz, 1948

Edith and Willy
Higuerote, Venezuela
Summer, 1952

Julius Foyer, Vienna 1939

Julius Foyer, Manila 1946

Mark Foyer, 1965

Mark Foyer, 2007

Mark, Willy and Edith, 1966
(before Willy's departure for college)

Willy and Susan on their wedding day
San Mateo, December 22, 1973

Edith, Julius and new grandson Carl
Seattle, 1982

With Julius in Alaska, 1994

On the Li River, China, 2001

Antarctica, 2002

Iguazu Falls, Brazil, 2002

Jerusalem, 2004

**With grandson Max
at his graduation from
Claremont McKenna College, 2006**

**Max and Carl
with their father, Willy**

VENEZUELA

MOVING TO VENEZUELA

Finally we had our papers in order and we were able to leave La Paz.

The last thing I remember of La Paz was my father holding the baby at the airport, as he had a very hard time letting him go. After all, we had stayed with my parents for close to two months. My parents were very fond of Willy and in reality they did not know when they would see him again. Although Karl said if things worked out as we hoped, we would return in a year to visit them, the thought of missing watching him grow made them very sad.

When we boarded the plane, we noticed a lady who looked European, like ourselves. She introduced herself as Thea Grunspan and told us she was also from Vienna and lived in Caracas. She was visiting her family in Cochabamba and was returning home. She originally had intended to leave Bolivia a few days earlier, but the travel agent who arranged her flight to Caracas was too lazy to book the same route for two different parties, so she was put on the same plane with us. If ever there was a happy coincidence to meet somebody, this was it. As you will see later, she and her husband helped us, and later myself, like we were close relatives.

Our first stop was Lima, Peru. We had a long layover and our good friends the Kronbergers from La Paz, who had moved to Lima a few years before, picked us up in their car, and invited Mrs. Grunspan to join us. She later often mentioned to me that she never forgot this hospitality. The Kronbergers showed us a little of Lima and then we went to their home, where I was able to boil some water and to prepare powdered milk for Willy to give him during the flight. I was also able to prepare some solid food for him. We had to change planes again in Panama City where there was another long layover. Finally we boarded the plane for our destination, La Guaira, Venezuela.

Avenida Bolívar   Caracas

Caracas, c. 1950

We were supposed to be picked up by a representative of the company, but due to a mix-up with the itinerary, the representative was not there to meet us. We expected a note indicating which hotel the company had made reservations for us. However, we did not see any note directed to us, so we went to the Hotel Ambassador, which Mrs. Grunspan had recommended and was close to where she lived. The Hotel Ambassador was not the only hotel in Caracas, but turned out to be the same hotel where the office of Sudamtex had made reservations for us—you can

imagine how surprised we were. While having break-
fast the next day, we got a call from the office wel-
coming us.

We stayed a few days in Caracas. During this
time Karl got instructions from the company to familiarize him with their policies and way of working. It
also gave me time to see a physician for Willy.
Through a friend of Mrs. Grunspan, I got the address
of a very good pediatrician.

You may note that I always referred to Mrs.
Grunspan by her last name. In South America we
seldom addressed people by their first name—it was
the same way as in Europe (or used to be), especially
when they were older than ourselves. Only after a long
friendship were you on a first-name basis with someone.

The doctor was from Barcelona, Spain. He was
living in Caracas for political reasons. He was very
interested meeting us, especially a child born in this
altitude by European parents. By the time we arrived
in Caracas, Willy was eleven months old and did not
stand up, which was, in La Paz, normal for children of
European parents. After being in Caracas for three
days, he was standing up and shortly afterwards he was
walking. I did not know anything about American
baby food. The physician informed me about the use
of canned baby food and how to take care of a baby in
the tropics. He also wrote down what to expect about
the baby's development. I used the information he
gave me for the whole year while we were living in
Maracay, as there were no competent pediatricians
there. I always said that if Willy got sick, I would have
to go to Caracas. Even if the advice of Dr. Spock were

available then, I would not have understood reading it, as my English was not good enough to follow instructions.

BEGINNING OUR LIFE IN MARACAY

The station wagon from the factory took us to Maracay and the hotel where we were supposed to stay. It took about four hours and the trip was very comfortable, as in general the highways were very good in Venezuela. When we arrived at the hotel, we found out that the office in Caracas had not made any arrangements for us with regard to our lodging. The hotel was completely occupied and Maracay did not have another hotel. As the factory had a permanent room at the hotel we were able to use this room until another room became available. After a few days we were able to move to our own room.

Hotel Jardín in Maracay

When I first saw the hotel, I was very impressed by it. It was originally built by the Venezuelan dictator

Juan Vicente Gomez (1908-1935). He also built the freeways. His plans were to make Maracay the capital of Venezuela. He ordered the building of this hotel and some military installations. The hotel itself was located on a beautiful landscaped square with a big fountain. On the other side of the square was a military school for cadets. The hotel had a tennis court, a swimming pool and a big garden, which was not too well kept. The disadvantages I found out later. The cheapest rooms were on the ground floor and the only way to get fresh air in those rooms was by the door leading toward an open corridor. In the tropical heat without air-conditioning, it was uncomfortable and dark. The rooms on the top floor were under the roof and the roof was not too well insulated. The result was that the rooms were very hot. In addition, those rooms were also smaller and did not have a small entrance room, as did the rooms on the ground and middle floors. As it was customary in Maracay, no house had glass windows, only screens to keep insects out.

Despite the greater expense of being in the middle, we decided to move to this floor. It had a very big room with a balcony and we were able to put Willy's playpen on the balcony. More importantly, the room had cross ventilation when we opened the door to the open corridor. It was like a veranda with comfortable chairs and you could socialize with the other people in the hotel. For the small room, I rented, through the factory, a refrigerator. There was a table, chairs and some cooking facilities so I could prepare meals for Willy, as I did not feel comfortable giving him hotel food.

The hotel served three meals daily in a very

attractive dining room. The ceiling was held up by columns and had no walls, so there was very good cross ventilation if there was a breeze. At the beginning, I liked the food very much. Lunch and dinner was a five-course affair, but there was no selection and they repeated more or less the same menu week after week. The dining room had a dress code. For dinner men had to wear a jacket or coat and women were not allowed into the dining room with sleeveless dresses. Although it was usually very hot, the men never took off their jackets when sitting down at the table. In spite of being in the tropics, neither men nor women wore shorts in the hotel.

I prepared Willy's food in our room and the discovery of canned baby food was a very big help. When I was more familiar with the hotel and at the advice of our waiter, I went to the hotel kitchen for different kinds of vegetables, eggs and chicken parts, which I was able to prepare for Willy. Sometimes our waiter brought a chicken to our room, which I was able to cook for us to have some change in our menu.

As much as I always have liked to play tennis, in Maracay I never went to the tennis court, as it was much too hot to play, although some people used the courts as early as six o'clock in the morning. The swimming pool was only filled with water for the weekend and as the pool did not have any filter, by Monday it did not look very inviting.

In Maracay and the surrounding area, there was no danger of malaria as this was very well controlled. Often in the early morning we saw big yellow trucks leaving the area carrying some insecticide against malaria. In all the years we lived in Venezuela there was only one outbreak of a tropical disease. While I was living in Caracas, yellow fever occurred in some province. There were enough vaccinations available

Swimming pool at Hotel Jardín

that everyone got vaccinated, although you had to stand in line. With regard to smallpox, which at this time was still a serious threat, sanitation workers regularly visited some barrios and vaccinated people free of charge.

In the hotel I still had some surprises in store. I found in the bathroom a dark brown insect of an inch or bigger (at least it looked to me that big) crawling in the bathroom. I called the office of the hotel and when the employee came, he was laughing, saying it was only a "cucaracha" or cockroach. I had never seen one before in La Paz—it was either too cold, or because of the lack of oxygen they were not able to live there. My second discovery was a spider. I had seen spiders before, but never this size. The lady who lived next to us informed me that they were completely harmless—in fact, they took care of insects. I had only to watch out if the spider was covered with hair. Those were very poisonous and called "black widows."

Even with the more expensive room, we had figured out that with all the meals covered, we should be able to save some money, but we did not realize that there were a lot of extra expenses—like tips for the waiter and room maids, extra food we had to buy for Willy and then all kinds of extras we didn't realize would add up. First, there was the laundry. At that time there were no disposable diapers or washing machines, so I washed them in the bathroom. I didn't want to give the baby's clothing to the hotel laundry. On our floor was an open space (actually it was the roof over the bar), where I could hang whatever I wanted to dry. In the heat, things dried very fast. In the beginning I had our clothes washed by the hotel, but later the ladies who lived on the same floor recommended a laundress who picked up the laundry and delivered it in a few days nice and clean—but it became quite expensive.

Not long after we moved to Maracay, we had a surprise visit from Mr. and Mrs. Grunspan. He was coming for a business meeting and she came along wanting to see us again and to find out how we were doing in our new surroundings. I was very happy to see them and also very glad to be able to speak German again, as in Bolivia we only conversed in German with our friends. She gave me all kinds of advice about living in the tropics. One thing she mentioned was about laundry—she told me that washing was very easy—to just buy a cake of blue soap, soap everything and leave it in the bathtub overnight and the next day you would just rinse everything. I had no experience with washing (I did not even know how to fold a shirt, as in La Paz the maid did all the laundry.)

I soaped everything, dark socks, white shirts, etc., and left it overnight in the bathtub and to my surprise, the dark socks faded and everything had dark spots. Naturally I was very desperate, seeing all the new white shirts and other clothing ruined. I was very lucky. Right after we arrived in Maracay, we met a couple, the Messners, who were from Brooklyn and about our age. The husband worked also for Sudamtex and soon after we became friends. When I showed Ruth Messner what happened to my laundry, she told me not to worry, as her husband was the chemist at the factory. She told me to give him everything and he would take care of it. I got everything back spot free. Later, I learned to iron shirts and I gave only bigger things to be washed.

I was very lucky to have Ruth in the hotel. Not only was she a good friend, but as my English was not very good when I arrived in Maracay, she was able to help me with my language skills. Her sister mailed her all kinds of American magazines, which I inherited, so I started to read in English with a dictionary. Unfortunately, she hated Maracay and was always dreaming of having a tomato and lettuce sandwich, which for health reasons we avoided eating. A few months after we arrived in Maracay she found out that she was expecting a baby and she returned to the States, with her husband following her shortly after.

Main street in Maracay, 1949

LIVING IN MARACAY

Sudamtex, the company where Karl was employed, was self-sufficient and able to produce the complete manufacture of cloth. This meant there was one department for spinning, one for weaving, one for dying and one for printing. Around Maracay, there were cotton fields and that cotton was used in the factory for the manufacture of cotton cloth. Besides this, there was a small department for the manufacture of rayon. Later, the company opened a factory for ready-made clothing in Los Teques, located in the cooler mountains halfway between Caracas and Maracay.

In Los Teques was a little boarding house owned by Austrian refugees. When we were living in Caracas, we spent lots of Sundays there. Even later when I was alone and was able to drive the mountain road myself, I went there often with Willy as he had children to play with and I met many good friends.

When we arrived in Maracay the factory was just recently built. Many of those in management had been there from the beginning, and along with most of the technical personnel, were primarily from the southern United States, where the big cotton mills were located. It seemed that the management felt they could use whatever practices they could get away with. For example, while the machinery was first class and the factory even had their own power plant, there was no air conditioning installed in spite of being in the tropics. This made working conditions very harsh for the workers. In addition, the general manager of the mill was never interested in learning Spanish. He said that since we paid the workforce, they should accommodate us and learn English. (He really used stronger language to express that.) This was naturally not very good for public relations, or employee morale.

The factory was in production twenty-four hours a day, and Karl was in charge of the weaving department for the second shift. This meant he left right after lunch and for dinner the car from the factory brought him to the hotel and then picked him up again. Other people living in the hotel and working at the same time went together in the car.

For Karl, this was a very big change. First, the climate was very different. La Paz was cold and Maracay very tropical and hot, especially in the factory, where the accumulated cotton dust from the machinery made you feel the heat more. In La Paz, he was the only boss but here there were other people with whom he had to share his opinion and learn the American way of working. He believed that the factory could be more productive if they changed the radius between weavers and mechanics. In this respect, in La Paz, Karl was very successful, as the Latinos working mentality was different from that of North American workers. When the CEO from the Caracas home office came for a regular inspection, Karl had a conference with him and tried to explain this. He suggested that Karl should make a report and that he would study it. During the mornings when Karl was not in the factory he worked very hard on the report. It had to be in English and at that time our English was not very good. Karl was very proud when he handed the report over and believed they would make some use of it. I doubt that anyone ever read it. At least, we never found out if they were interested enough to use some of his suggestions. As one can understand, Karl was not happy with this, as he felt the people in the mill did not appreciate what he had to give.

Also, privately, it was very difficult for both of us. Besides having our families in Bolivia we were used to associating mostly with German-speaking Jewish people. In Maracay, there were none. There were some Jewish families who had stores and who had been living there for many years and whom I believe were very wealthy, but they were much older than we. Later one family moved to Caracas and owned a big bookstore, but I never had any social contact with them. When Karl passed away, they visited me and asked if they could help, but there was not much they could do. The older Jewish families even founded a club in Maracay where we assumed they went mostly for gambling. We went once to the club during Passover. There were candles lit in the so-called temple and they had even a Torah scroll, but in the room in front of it a card game was taking place. We were so disappointed that this was the only time we went there.

We found one couple our age. The wife was from New York and they had a little boy and sometimes we met. They had a car, although she did not drive, and sometimes in the evening they picked us up and we went for a little drive outside of Maracay. She was a nice person, only she believed when leaving her house she had to dress up and nobody dressed up—for instance, nobody wore stockings in Maracay, it was much too hot for it. They visited me shortly after Karl died and told me that they were getting a divorce, which did not surprise me, as she always felt she was too good to spend her life in Maracay.

During the time we lived at the hotel, General Electric was building a power plant nearby and the top personnel lived at the hotel. I could converse in English, but especially in the beginning, I had some difficulties, and so it took me some time until I felt comfortable enough to talk to them. There were some very interesting people living on the same floor. One couple I found out worked for General Electric during the thirties in Russia, or Siberia, and the wife, who had time while living in the hotel, had written a book about her experiences. Next door to us was an elderly couple. He worked in the tobacco fields. They were childless and she was from Southern California, as she was always telling me how she missed the vegetables and fruits from there, especially cauliflower. She was a very nice neighbor. Whenever we wanted to go to a movie she watched Willy. In general, the people who worked for General Electric had grown children in the United States but liked to work overseas, because those jobs were very well paid and they could save money.

Not only did I have difficulty with my English, I suddenly also had a problem with my Spanish. The Bolivians spoke in general a very clear Spanish and slowly as everything, due to the altitude, was slow. In Venezuela, the Spanish was spoken very fast and often the end syllables were ignored. Some fruits had completely different names. Frankly, at the beginning I was so unhappy there that I was not even interested in understanding everything. I missed my family and the friends we had in La Paz, and was actually homesick for Bolivia.

The married couples who worked for Sudamtex

were mostly there from the beginning and were able to find houses. The bachelors lived in the hotel like us and as there was not much to do on the weekends, they spent most of their time in the bar. We did not have much private contact with the married couples from Sudamtex. They had different interests. Besides we did not have a car and walking to their houses was too far, especially in the heat. There was one young couple who had a small child and the wife invited me to visit her one morning. When I arrived at her place, the first thing she offered me was a Cuba Libre, a cocktail made with rum. Coca-Cola I would have liked, but at eleven o'clock in the morning I was not ready for a Cuba Libre. We didn't visit each other often after that.

As employees of Sudamtex, we had the privilege of the occasional use of their station wagon and the driver. One Sunday we took the opportunity to drive to the beach and some other employees joined us for the trip. A well-paved two-way road took us to Ocumare beach. I don't know how long it took us to get there. The road went through a virgin rain forest and if you looked closely you could see wild orchids or other very interesting plants such as ferns clinging to the big trees.

One day a botanist arrived from the United States who had a special permit to collect all kinds of orchids and permission in the States to import them. It was interesting to see how he packed those plants for transport, making sure the plants didn't carry diseases that could infect other plants in the States. It was the first time Karl and I had ever been on a beach. Even without any experience swimming in the ocean, we enjoyed the big waves. Later we found out that although the beach was crowded, it was not safe to

Karl and Willy, April 1949

swim there and later when we were living in Caracas we avoided those kinds of beaches.

Close to Maracay was a big lake, Lago Valencia, and one Sunday a few single employees of the company went fishing. I don't know if they caught some fish, but they caught a four-foot-long alligator and deposited it in the bathtub of a friend. You can imagine how surprised this man was when he returned from a late night at the bar, stepped into the bathtub and found an alligator there. In the middle of the patio of the hotel was a fountain and the next day we found the alligator in the fountain and heard the whole story.

In Venezuela you could go to bullfights and

Maracay had a big bullring, built by the dictator Gomez. I didn't understand anything about bullfights but was told that in Caracas certain ways of killing the bull were not allowed, but in Maracay they were and very famous bullfighters came to Maracay. We naturally were not interested in bullfighting, but when the toreador did a good job, he was covered with flowers and carried on the shoulders of people to the hotel to celebrate his triumph, so we saw that. This was always a big event.

That was the entertainment we had in Maracay. Although there were some movie houses there and we had a very nice neighbor who offered to watch Willy if we felt like going, we did not want to take advantage of her offer and very seldom went.

At the beginning of our stay in Maracay we tried to find a house, but we realized that not having a car would make that impossible, as Karl would lose his transportation to and from the factory. Somehow we were not ready to buy a car. Karl started to learn to drive and we thought if we stayed in Maracay we would get a car, but our staying there was still questionable. As the price for gasoline was, and still is, very cheap in Venezuela, driving a car was not expensive; it just seemed like a big step for us.

Venezuelan families also lived in the hotel. I became close to one lady who had a child Willy's age and the children played together, as much as children at that age play together. I don't remember if I ever met her husband.

As long as Ruth was still in Maracay, she kept me supplied with American magazines, which I attempted to read with a dictionary, although it was very challenging and time-consuming. After awhile my English improved enough that I could make sense of the articles and then seldom needed a dictionary. I also received daily a newspaper from Caracas in Spanish and dreamed about how nice it would be to live there. Later, the office in the hotel had paperback books in English for sale and I bought a couple. Those were actually the first books I read in the English language. My first one was, <u>Mr. Blondie Builds His Dream House</u>, or something similar. Even now if I need some mayor repairs in my house I am careful with reading the different estimates, thanks to this book. The second book was <u>The Egg and I</u>. Later a TV series was based on this book. I also learned something from this book. The author was living in the state of Washington on a chicken farm, producing eggs, but she had no experience with cooking and baking. She often had cracked eggs, which could not be sold, so she used the extra eggs for baking and the cakes came out very well. In most cake recipes I had from Vienna I always added one extra egg and I believe it improved my cakes.

As mentioned before, when we arrived in Venezuela I visited a pediatrician and he gave me good information for Willy, but he never gave me any information what to do about heat rash. This was a big problem I had with Willy as he had it very badly. The ladies on our floor who had raised children before gave me all kinds of advice, but nothing helped and I tried everything. In spite of that, I gave him a bath twice a day, using all kinds of powders and creams. It looked so bad, that when I walked with him on the street, people mentioned, "What a poor child—the mother takes him out when he has the measles."

Apparently it did not bother the baby, because he did not scratch it and did not show in any way that it bothered him. The heat rash only went away when we moved to Caracas. Once Willy had what I thought was a cold. In the hotel lived an American doctor and I asked him for any advice. He just came to the door and told me to give him vitamin C and that he would get well. We did not use vitamins in Bolivia and definitely not as a cure against a cold. Later I found out that the doctor I had asked was working for the Rockefeller Institute for mosquito control and malaria prevention. He was definitely not a pediatrician.

Actually we were lucky with the timing of our arrival in Maracay, because January was the coldest month of the year. However, it still felt very hot for us. It only cooled down early in the morning, about five o'clock. The worst month was May before the rainy season started. When it started to rain it cooled off a little bit, but then the humidity was worse. Sometimes wind came before or followed the rain and that helped. When it is very windy here in California I very seldom complain, as we looked forward to even a small breeze there. Shortly after we arrived in Maracay we bought an electric fan and put it close to the window, but it never really cooled the air.

Sometimes before the rain started, the sky was very dark, more like black, and you could see big swarms of yellow butterflies. They were like clouds against the dark sky and green trees and were quite a sight. The rain never lasted very long—it was more like a cloudburst and even if you were just was crossing the street you got drenched.

During Spring some trees had beautiful purple

blossoms. Unfortunately at that time we did not have color film, so we were unable to capture the wonderful colors. I especially remember that in Caracas we also had some purple blooming trees with green foliage in the springtime, while in Maracay there were trees with purple blooms without foliage that looked like big flower bouquets.

GETTING RESTLESS IN MARACAY

While I was living in Venezuela telephone communications between cities was difficult. There was so much static noise that you could hardly hold a conversation. In addition, it was also very expensive. The Hotel Jardín where we lived had a telephone in the office, but we never thought to use it as we did not know anyone to call. I don't even know if it was available for guests except in case of emergency. A few years ago, when I was visiting Venezuela, everybody had a cell phone. Things had really changed.

Aside from the mail there was practically no other way to communicate. That may sound strange now. There were two ways to mail letters. One was by airmail—for that you used only a very thin onion paper, because the weight of the letter was very much controlled. Mail sent by regular transport was cheaper but often took a long time to reach the destination. While I was working in Caracas, office mail was always sent by airmail and later copies by regular mail, to be sure that no mail got lost. You could also use telegrams. Use of those was very expensive, as you had to pay for every word, and not very practical.

After living a short time in Maracay, we found out that my sister-in-law Mathi had a cousin living in Caracas with her husband. One day we had a nice surprise, as they had a car and were able visit us. They were happy to find some family members, even very distantly related, as they had no other relatives there. Hanna, especially, considered us family. Although Hanna had brothers living in England, they were far away and they could only have contact with them by mail. For this reason, they felt very lonely. Unfortunately, due to a misunderstanding we did not see much of them in Caracas. Both were survivors from the concentration camp Theresienstadt. Later they moved to Seattle, Washington. After Hanna's husband passed away, she moved to Los Angeles, to be close to Mathi's sister. I visited Hanna there several times and celebrated her ninetieth birthday with her a few years ago. I stayed in close contact with her until she passed away.

During July 1949 I received news from La Paz that my father had a heart attack. After a few weeks of bed rest, he was again able to lead a normal life. (My father lived twenty-seven years more.) My parents did not want to wait for a second attack, as living in the alti-tude of La Paz was very hard on the heart, and wanted to leave La Paz. My father had a customer who was the Consul or Ambassador of the United States, who had suggested to my father that he should move to the United States because of the excellent work my father did. He even brought my father the necessary papers to apply for an emigration visa. My father filled the pa-pers out, more to satisfy a customer, but later it was a very good coincidence that my father applied for the visa at that time. My father had lived in the States in 1909, so it was familiar to him.

At the same time, we came to the conclusion that we did not want to spend the rest of our lives in Maracay. In listening to the people in the hotel how beautiful life was in the United States, we decided it might be a good idea to try to move there too. Ruth was always craving tomato and lettuce sandwiches in

Brooklyn where she had kept a kosher house, although her dreaming of those sandwiches may have been because she was pregnant at that time. Different Americans living in the hotel were always talking about the wonderful produce, meat and food that in general was available in the States, so that you really felt like you wanted to taste it. A college friend of Karl's in the factory described to us the beautiful mountains of Tennessee and told us that whenever we came to the States we should never miss visiting there. Since living in the States, I have visited many beautiful parks and mountain ranges; unfortunately, I never went to Tennessee. All this convinced us that life in the States must be nice and we decided that we would try to apply for a visa. The United States had a quota system for immigration, accepting people based on where they were born. Someone had to guarantee that they would take care of you and that you would not be a burden to the country, or you must show that you had enough money to be independent. As we both were born in Vienna, we were informed it would take a few years until our number came up, but we registered anyway. It was a good thing we did, because my quota number came due in 1956. I was grateful for that, as it gave me the freedom to make decisions with every option available.

When Karl went to Caracas to the American Embassy he combined it with a visit to our friends, the Grunspans, asking them if there might be a chance that he could get a job in Caracas. Both of us did not like living in Maracay, and we were not sure if Karl would get his contract renewed. The company had contacted us, but did not confirm anything. Mr. Grunspan suggested that Karl put an ad in the local paper and see what would happen. We did not expect much, but to our surprise in a short while we got an answer to the ad informing us that a new factory was being built in the suburbs of Caracas and they were looking to hire people with Karl's experience. When Karl received this offer, we decided we would all go to Caracas and find out more. I was really anxious to go and see more of Caracas after living almost a year in the interior. I thought I might even be able to meet some people besides the Grunspans with a European background.

At that time you could travel to Caracas by reserving just one seat in a taxi, which was a less expensive way to make the trip. So we returned to our old Hotel Ambassador. The whole trip took about four hours. In Maracay, due to the heat, there were no glass windows, only screens against mosquitoes or other flying insects and wooden shutters. Willy had never seen a window before, and he was kept busy by looking through the glass and wondering why he was not being able to put his hands through.

The offer of the job seemed reasonable to us. By that time we were already used to the expensive living in Venezuela. Karl's salary was to be in Bolivars, in contrast to Karl's payment at Sudamtex, which was in U.S. dollars, but the Bolivar was very strong. It was one of the few South American countries that had no restriction with regard to sending or receiving foreign currency. While in Maracay we opened an account at a bank in New York and Karl had his salary deposited there and we were always hoping to increase the amount later. With our experience with the devaluation of the Bolivar in Bolivia, we wanted to keep a nest egg in America. One plus of the job was that it included an apartment in the factory. As it was shortly after the war and there was a lot of immigration, there was an acute housing shortage in Caracas.

When Karl had signed the new contract and notified the company and his boss, they were disappointed because the company was very satisfied with the way Karl worked; but we had finally had enough of life in Maracay and hotel life with a small child.

ON THE MOVE TO CARACAS

Tocome was the name of the company that hired Karl. It was built and owned by Mr. Diaberikian, who was Armenian, as was the general manager. By the time Karl was hired, the company had already hired an American who used to live in Havana and was married to a Cuban. The couple had a girl who was five years old and as we became neighbors we became friends. Later the company hired some more new employees from different countries: an Italian for the weaving department, a nice Bulgarian couple for the chemical department, and another Italian for the spinning department. The electric plant was managed by people from the United States. Those in management, as well as the workers, were of mixed nationalities, and we all got along well. During that time there was a very big influx of immigrants from Italy and Italian was the second language spoken in the factory. The factory, like the one in Maracay, had departments for spinning, weaving and dying cloth and they also constructed their own power plant, so we had always electricity.

Karl was supposed to start working early in January, when the construction of the factory was finished. By that time we would be able to move into our apartment, which was supposed to be furnished. We had our own beds, which we brought from Bolivia, and all our belongings were still stored in the factory in Maracay. Once we had our apartment, everything was going to be shipped to us in Caracas.

We left Maracay during November for a little vacation in Macuto, a vacation spot on the beach.

182

It was about one hour away from Caracas, depending on the traffic. It was one of the few places that had decent hotels. Macuto, being located at the beach, was also very warm, so after a short time we decided to move to Los Teques while waiting until Karl could start work. Los Teques, located in the mountains about halfway between Maracay and Caracas, was much in higher altitude, and much cooler than both places. We knew of a small boarding house there that was owned and managed by two Austrian sisters and their families. One of the sisters was a survivor from Auschwitz.

In Los Teques, Willy finally got rid of his heat rash and there I also started giving him normal food. Prior to this, in Maracay, I was afraid to give him any hotel food. The owners of the boarding house prepared proper food for Willy. They also had a little girl, but she was a few years older than Willy. In the boarding house, we met a couple, Mr. and Mrs. Bern, whom Karl knew from Ecuador. They also lived temporarily in Los Teques as at that time there was a housing shortage in Caracas. I was not sure if they were thinking of staying in Venezuela. They had left Ecuador because Mr. Bern thought there were better business opportunities in Venezuela. They had a five-year-old daughter, whom Willy adored. As long as I lived in Venezuela, I met them frequently and later Lilly, their daughter, moved to California and for many years we stayed in contact, until she moved east.

Finally, in Los Teques, I had contact again with Austrian and German-speaking people and I felt very comfortable there. Many people who were originally from Austria liked to come visit this place to cool off and meet friends and have European food.

The Jewish population of Caracas consisted of old timers, mainly Sephardic Jews, who had lived in Venezuela for generations, as well as new refugees who fled Europe in the 1930s. Caracas had a very beautiful synagogue built by the Sephardic Jews, which I visited once. The new generation of refugees didn't have very much contact with the old timers. Only the next generation intermarried. The new refugees, mostly of German and Polish descent who arrived in the mid-1930s, were mostly Austrian Jews, actually from Vienna, and arrived on one ship. It is quite a story how they were able to come to Venezuela, which was made into a movie, The Voyage of the Damned. I was told that the people left on a ship from Hamburg, Germany, destination unknown, hoping some island in the Caribbean or the United States would allow them to land and to settle. In every port they tried to land, they were refused until their last hope was Venezuela.

The Sephardic colony heard about their plight. As they were very influential in Venezuela, they were able to make arrangements for the people to land. So that the population would not be aware of the sudden influx of German-speaking people, the passengers had to leave the ship during the night and were transported to several places close to Caracas. From there, they were slowly integrated in the Caracas population. It was a very happy ending for them. However, a second ship arrived later and the people were not able to land and the ship returned to Germany. I don't know if the people survived. Tragically, one gentleman, whom I didn't meet, saw his wife on the second ship and was unable to arrange for her to land.

Later, the Austrian colony was augmented with relatives who came from Shanghai and even some who survived the concentration camps in Germany. Most of the children were older than I was. One friend mentioned to me once that if he had had children, he would have been afraid to take such a risky journey with a small child. There were only a few people my age, whom I met later. While I was living in Caracas, the captain of the first ship came for a visit and you can imagine the reception he had when he arrived. He felt very happy that he was able to save the people and see them become successful.

When I arrived in Caracas, most of those passengers were well established, or at least I did not meet the other ones. Some had retail businesses, while others had import companies. Since Venezuela had not much industry and even had to import food, importing was a big business in Venezuela. Some were employed by big companies or by other refugees.

As the living quarters in the factory were not ready for us to use, we had to stay in a hotel until we were able to occupy the apartment. As I felt comfortable with the baby in Los Teques and did not like the idea of going back to feeding Willy out of baby food cans, we decided the best thing would be for me to stay in Los Teques until we would be able to move into the apartment. In the meantime, Karl would stay in the hotel in Caracas and come on weekends to see us. Once the apartment was ready, we would give the order to the factory in Maracay to send our crates to Caracas.

The first news Karl brought me of the apartment was that it was very small, but we were really looking forward to have our own apartment, so we said never mind for the beginning. As the factory was still under construction, we might be able to get a bigger apartment later.

The other interesting news was that the machinery for the factory was quite different from the ones they had in Maracay, which were very modern. Here there were reconstructed machines and second-hand looms. The crates were stored outside during the construction of the factory, which was during the rainy season. When the crates were opened, water ran out and everything was rusty; but with a lot of cleaning and elbow grease, after a while the machines were running and produced decent merchandise.

A few days before we were able to occupy the apartment, we asked a man in the factory in Maracay to ship our belongings from the factory to Caracas. At the same time I went to Caracas and spent a few days in the hotel to prepare for our move. The apartment was really very small. It had a small living room, a bedroom of somewhat better size and a very small kitchen and bathroom. I always said I should not get pregnant or gain a lot of weight while living in this apartment, because I would not be able to open the door to the refrigerator. The apartment was on the second floor and on the ground floor we shared a washing machine with our neighbor. Although I was already familiar with a refrigerator, I had never seen a washing machine before.

Our neighbor was actually Karl's boss. Because he was hired before Karl, their apartment was bigger and also had an entrance hall and a big balcony. There was a second building with a bigger apartment with four bedrooms, but this was reserved for bachelors. In this building was also a nice apartment, occupied by the chemist and his wife, who were acquaintances of the owner who was originally from Bulgaria. The wife was often very lonely and we visited each other often.

The personnel were very international, like a little United Nations, and we all got along well. The third man in the weaving department, the Italian, who was an experienced cook, did the cooking for the bachelors. The other two men in the apartment were from the United States and were in charge of installing the power plant and keeping it working. The fourth man in this apartment was a very young man, also from Italy. He was in charge of the spinning department. The Italian who was a good cook tried to teach me how to make real Italian spaghetti. Although I followed his instructions very carefully, my spaghetti tasted more like a Viennese goulash.

When I started to unpack our belongings, I quickly realized that I would be unable to store everything I had shipped. Not only I had packed everything that I owned in La Paz, I had bought new pots and pans. As I mentioned earlier, I thought in Venezuela I would not be able to buy new things as it was shortly after the war and there was still a shortage of certain merchandise. In Caracas everything was available and of much better quality than the merchandise in Bolivia. In addition, I had a lot of things that Karl's mother brought from Vienna. Some were very useful to us; some were antiques, which I treasured and still have. But I had things for which I did not have any use at that time and I was sure that I would not need—like a hood you put over a stove for baking. For my first few cakes in La Paz, I used this contraption and I was even able to bake a cake, which was edible, but having now a normal stove with an oven, I was convinced that I would never miss this hood, which took a lot of space, so I discarded it right away.

The factory was located in the outskirts of Caracas, not in the industrial area, but close to the residential area. There were no stores within walking distance, so I had to take public transportation for whatever I needed. I got bread delivered regularly. In the suburbs, as well as in some parts of Caracas, vegetable farmers came with little horse-drawn carts offering their produce. These farmers were from Portugal and grew their crops in fields close to Caracas. The big supermarkets delivered everything. I enjoyed going with Willy and exploring the supermarkets, where I saw merchandise completely unknown to me. I also enjoyed visiting downtown Caracas and getting to know the city. Not too far from where we lived I found a little private park for children, where you paid a monthly fee. There I met other mothers with little children and almost all of them were from Europe.

A few weeks after we had moved to the apartment, on a Sunday afternoon just before we intended to go out, Willy slipped in the bathroom and cried very hard. We were afraid that he had injured himself. As it was Sunday, the pediatrician was not available, so we took a taxi to the hospital. As we were new in the city, we asked the taxi driver to take us to an emergency room. He suggested the Red Cross Hospital, which was free. We did not like the idea of a charity hospital. We asked the driver if there is not another one for first aid. He suggested the Medical Center, which was the biggest and best hospital in Caracas. It was a Sunday afternoon and the doctor on duty was some intern. He told us that a child under two years of age did not break bones because they are too soft. We believed him and went home. With Willy I never had trouble with food—he ate everything I offered him and suddenly he refused to eat anything. Then there was something else we noticed. He was at an age when he enjoyed turning on the light switches and suddenly he refused to do it with one hand. After about one week our neighbor the Cuban lady noticed that on Willy's wrist was a little bump. By that time we were able to get the name of a bone specialist and took Willy to the specialist. He took some x-rays and told us Willy had a broken arm and the arm should be put in a cast, which he would have to wear for about three weeks. He wanted to check the arm again in a week or so. This doctor informed us that had we not noticed the break, it would probably have healed crooked and it would have been necessary to operate to straighten out the bone. So we were lucky. After a very short time Willy's appetite returned and he was a happy child again. The only thing that remained of this experience was that as the doctor wore a white coat and barbers in Caracas wore white coats, too, I had a hard time getting Willy to a barber for a haircut.

There was another kind of worry we had with Willy. He was nearly two years old and did not talk. The only words he said were, "Mama" and "Papa." He understood whatever we said to him in German, English and Spanish, and when he heard the workers of the factory speaking Italian I believe he understood Italian too. We took him to our pediatrician and he assured us that nothing was wrong. The problem was he heard too many different languages. He advised us that when he started to talk, we should answer in this language. He started with Spanish, so his mother tongue became Spanish. Although with Karl I spoke mostly German, for many years Willy understood German but never talked in German. When Willy graduated from college he went on the trip to Europe and also to Germany, where as he told us he could understand the people, but was not able to answer in German. The doctor told us that he had a nephew in Barcelona, where they speak Spanish and Catalan, who he did not talk until he was four years old and later became a well-known scientist.

The couple living next to us was very interesting. She was a Cuban and he was an American, much older than she. Actually, it was his second marriage and he had grown children in the States. His Spanish was very poor and so was her English. She often complained to me that Charlie did not talk much to her in the evenings, so she came over to us for company. After a while she made friends with people from Havana, then Charlie came over to our apartment when he felt lonely and spoke to Willy in English. No wonder that our child was very confused with the different languages.

When you had an apartment in a factory you socialized with your neighbors (as there was neither television nor computer for distraction, only a radio). Usually textile mills are never on main streets, so you were far from town. There were some advantages to living on the property of the factory, such as having people clean my windows and do other help in the apartment. The disadvantage was that Karl needed to be available on a twenty-four hour basis and was often called in the evening if there was a problem at the mill.

During June, Karl's brother Kurt visited us while on a business trip to the United States. On his return, he made a detour to see us. He told us that he'd had enough of living in La Paz and was looking for a country in South America with a decent climate and good living conditions where he could settle down. He visited Chile, Argentine, Uruguay and Peru. Brazil was out of the question, because of the different language. Finally he decided on Montevideo, Uruguay, where some of his friends from La Paz were already living.

After Kurt's visit, we decided to get a car. While living at the factory, you really were more or less always on duty, never knowing when you were going to be called in for an emergency or something else. Karl had already a driver's license from Maracay, so we started looking for a car. We were very lucky as we bought a two-door 1948 Chevrolet from the man who delivered our bread, as he wanted to buy himself a delivery truck. We assumed the car was in good shape and we never had any problems with it.

With the purchase of the car, we were no longer dependent on public transportation. As the factory was on the outskirts of Caracas, getting somewhere was sometimes difficult and very time consuming. A bigger problem was to find a taxi where we lived. Caracas did not have taxi stands, nor was it possible to order one by phone. Taxis cruised around and you just stopped one. It was often difficult for us because of where we lived.

We started with little Sunday excursions. At first we drove around the different suburbs, which were very beautiful. After Karl got more experience, sometimes we drove to Los Teques. There, we always met other German-speaking people, mostly Austrian refugees from Europe. Slowly we got acquainted with this group of people and many became good friends of ours. There was one couple, Mr. and Mrs. Sensel, who had a boy Willy's age and the children played together and later went to the same school. Sometimes we took our neighbors along, too. With them we went to a park, which was close to the boarding house.

We also drove to the beach, but this was quite a long drive on a very windy road, which sometimes was very foggy. We usually took a picnic along. We often bought fresh green coconuts on the beach, which the vendors opened with a machete. After we drank the refreshing coconut milk, they broke the nuts so we were able to eat the soft milky inside. On the way home, fishermen were standing along the road with fresh fish right from the boat. At first we were very tempted to buy this fresh fish, but to bring such a fish home was challenging. We were living in the tropics and it was always hot. The trip took, depending on traffic, between one to three hours and we did not have an ice chest, as this was unknown to us. We discovered that if you fastened the fish with a hook on the window, the fish did not spoil because the wind kept them cool. Everyone knew then that you were coming from the beach. I tried a few times to bring fish home in this way, but it was a lot of work to clean them, to get all the scales off and divide the fish and clean the insides. A few years later a very nice new highway was opened, which made the trip much shorter and less dangerous. The new highway was pleasant to drive and I did it sometimes with some friends, even after dinner.

Sometimes when Karl came home from work we went shopping, which made it easier for me, and also we were able to have more variety in our food. As in Bolivia, I always liked to explore and I enjoyed trying out new things, as some vegetables and fruits were unknown to me. We did not have things like broccoli, sweet potatoes, yams and eggplants in Europe, and definitely not in Bolivia. Having always lived in countries without access to the ocean I was not familiar with seafood, especially crab and shrimp. With the help of my Cuban neighbor and the Italian cook—I was a good student—we had a good variety of healthy food. In Venezuela, as in Bolivia, every vegetable or fruit we ate had to be boiled or peeled. The drinking water had to be boiled too. Only in the later years we were able to buy lettuce from the United States, which was very expensive. As much of the food was imported, living expenses were very high. For instance, in the tropics it was too hot to grow potatoes, so we had them imported from Holland. Also from Holland, we received butter and cheese. We received chickens and canned goods from the United States; all of which were better quality than what was produced locally. The meat I preferred to buy was imported from Argentina, as it was also of a better quality than the local products. You were also able to buy frozen food and TV dinners, but I never bought them, because I was not sure that the refrigeration during the transportation was adequate and some food might have arrived spoiled.

The best bananas I ate anywhere were in Venezuela. Lately in one of my travels to South America, I visited a banana plantation in Ecuador and was not able to get my kind of bananas. I was told they were too delicate for long transportation, so they didn't cultivate them for export. Perhaps in a local market I could have found the ones I liked so much. Oranges were better in Bolivia than in Venezuela. The climate could have been too hot for growing oranges. European fruits like apples, pears, and sometimes peaches, were available. But those fruits were imported and very expensive. You could find strawberries on the market, but you had to cook them. There were plenty of fruits we enjoyed very much, like papayas, mangos, pineapples and cherimoyas. There was also a special kind of corn on the cob. The cobs were relatively small and the kernels were pointed and very sweet. Corn was very popular and consumed widely by the Venezuelans. They made many things from corn flour, including special rolls called arrepas, which could be sliced in half, buttered, filled with ham, heated and eaten like a sandwich. If you had household help, with every meal you had to include baked or fried bananas (platanos), rice and black beans.

There was another advantage living in a factory: if we wanted to go out in the evening to a movie or show, we asked somebody from the factory to watch Willy and we knew he would be in good hands.

Once Karl felt secure in driving, he suggested I should learn to drive too. To get a driver's license in Caracas was no big problem, but to be able to drive you had to have a certificate from a physician that you were physically capable to drive and this certificate had to be renewed every year. It was a very nice income for doctors. Our car had a manual transmission, as did all cars at that time, so it was more difficult to learn to drive. Karl really had patience in teaching me to drive, although as long as he lived I never drove by myself, only on more or less deserted streets with him sitting next to me.

For New Years 1950-1951 we decided to get away from the factory for a little while, so we returned to the hotel in Macuto where we had been when we left the factory in Maracay before moving to Caracas. It was a nice change. It was very warm being on the beach, but for a few days we enjoyed it, for being the winter month of December, the heat was not too bad.

CHANGING JOBS
AND MOVING TO A RENTED HOUSE

After Karl was working at the Tocome factory for more than one year, he was approached by Mr. Zander, a German refugee who had left Europe in the early 1930s and who founded an import company. He also acted as an agent for different industries. They had a special department of supplies for the textile industry, which they wanted to enlarge. Up until then, Mr. Scharf, an Austrian refugee from Vienna, took care of this department, but he was also overseeing other parts of the office. They were looking for someone to be in charge of the textile department with knowledge of the textile industry. He must also be able to visit factories in the interior, like the old Sudamtex factory in Maracay. I believe there were a few more factories in the interior, so it was important that the employee had his own car. It was also required that the person working in the textile department be able to act as a troubleshooter and for this you had to have a thorough knowledge of every aspect of running a textile factory. Mr. Zander offered Karl a salary that we considered adequate as a starting salary. By that time we were already used to the high living expenses in Venezuela. Besides, Karl was getting tired working in factories, which was also physically demanding. He thought it was time to change to office work and with Willy growing the apartment in the factory was really getting too small. By that time his brother Kurt had moved to Montevideo, Uruguay, and had opened an office there. There was the possibility that the brothers might work together in the future and that office experience would be helpful.

When we left Maracay during November of 1949, not long after the war, there was a big shortage of apartments in Caracas. But now there was a lot of construction and apartments were available. We were lucky to find a house in a residential area, which was not too far from the center where the office was located. Karl was able to come home for lunch, which we actually considered our main meal. As most offices and many stores closed at noon, the worst traffic problem of the whole day was around this time. In the evening stores and offices closed at different times there was usually no problem with commuting.

The house was located on a one-block street and on the same street lived a few little boys the same age as Willy, so he had enough playmates. As the only traffic in the street was from neighbors, the boys could play safely on the street. In front of the house was a little yard, which Karl really enjoyed, as it reminded him of the house he had to leave in Vienna. In Caracas, when you rented a house, it was completely empty. The bathroom had the essentials and the kitchen had only a sink. So before moving, we had to buy a refrigerator, stove and also a water heater. In the factory we had an electric stove, but this time we decided on gas, for the stove and the water heater. The gas we got delivered in special butane gas tanks and we always got it replaced without any trouble. As Venezuela is a country with plenty of oil, gas was also cheap for household use, cheaper than electricity. We only had the beds, which we had brought from Bolivia. Now we had to buy furniture and some kitchen cabinets. The house had three bedrooms, a living and dining room, a very large kitchen and also a little extra bathroom for household help. In Venezuela, houses seldom had bathtubs, only showers. Floors were usually some kind of granite or stone or as in our house, tile, which had to be washed with water a few times a week. To this we added kerosene, to avoid infestation of little critters, like cucarachas, etc.

A few blocks away from the house was a tennis and swim club, which we joined. In many South American countries a lot of social life took place in private clubs. The Casa Blanca Club, which we joined, was more a sport club, where Willy learned to swim. Sometimes the club also hosted parties for children, especially during the Carnival season. Our biggest interest in joining the club was that a lot of members were Austrian refugees and we really wanted to get in contact with "landsmen," something we missed very much in Maracay. Before joining our club, the only contact we had with German-speaking Europeans was when we drove to the boarding house in Los Teques. Few of the adults went swimming—it was more for socializing, so the pool was used mostly by the children and the young people. As I always liked very much to swim, I took advantage of the pool. Some of the adults played tennis and took the game very seriously and did not invite newcomers. Only much later did I find a partner with whom I met in the evening to play.

It was really very fortunate that Karl had changed his job at this time, as my parents wrote that their quota number became due and with this they had the permission to immigrate to the United States. My father, after his heart attack, did not want to live in the altitude of La Paz any longer. As my father had lived in New York during 1908 and 1909, he felt he was coming home, and did not consider his age a difficulty. At this time he was only sixty-eight years old and he lived to age ninety-two.

On the way to New York, my parents definitely wanted to see us and spend some time with us. My mother also wrote that they had found an aunt; actually a cousin of my father's, living in New York. How they found Aunt Ella, as I called her, I don't know. I believe at that time you could make searches through some Jewish German newspapers in New York. When we left Vienna, Aunt Ella was supposed to go to England as a household maid—at that time this was the only way to get an entry visa to England. Her husband and my cousin, with whom I was very close, were able to cross together illegally to Belgium with the two brothers of Aunt Ella. I never found out how the whole family made it to the United States. Her brothers were Dr. Fritz and Dr. Max Beckmann, mentioned previously, also living in New York with their wives. I assumed their wives made it out of Austria via England, where they worked as household maids. When I arrived in New York in 1956, both brothers were practicing again as physicians.

My parents came to Caracas during the summer of 1951. It was a very happy reunion. The last time they saw Willy, he was a baby. Now he was a little boy with whom they could play and talk. As we had a car, we took them to Los Teques, where they met some of our acquaintances and also saw the beach. As my parents had always lived in inland countries, they enjoyed the visit to the beach very much. After we had moved to Venezuela, they had gone on vacations with Lilly, Ernst and Freddie to the port of Arica, Chile.

I took my father downtown to some jewelry stores. We tried to convince my parents to stay with us in Caracas where we were living and not go to New York. They would actually be alone in New York. They did not know how Aunt Ella and Uncle Ernst Discant, who were living in New York, had changed during the war years and how they were now after so many years. Besides my father was not so young anymore. However, after seeing the work in the different jewelry stores, my father decided this was not a place for him. Better gold jewelry was sometimes higher priced, but in general everything was priced according to weight. Also, the hot, tropical climate bothered my father.

After about one month with us, we took my parents to the airport and notified Aunt Ella when my parents would arrive in New York. Telephone connections to the United States were very difficult at the time, and besides we did not have a telephone in our house. My parents promised that they would send us a cable upon arrival. Unfortunately, my parents had some problems when arriving in New York. At that time, also when I immigrated to the United States a few years later, you had to have proof that you had no tuberculosis or any other contagious disease. You had to have x-rays of your lungs and a health certificate issued by a physician of the American Embassy. Somehow the x-rays of my father were not clear and they had to spend a few days on Ellis Island. Right away, my parents contacted my aunt, who actually was waiting for them at the airport. She was able, with the help of a lawyer, to arrange for my parents to leave Ellis Island within a few days. There was nothing wrong with my father's x-rays, just a misunderstanding.

Karl liked the change in his professional life very much. We soon realized, however, that living expenses were much higher than we expected. Now we had to pay rent and electricity, which we did not have to pay living at the factory. I also needed some help in the house. In Venezuela it was not like living in the U.S. where you got everything packaged or cleaned. For this reason everything took much more time to prepare. Like in Bolivia, you had to be very careful with the preparation of food, where everything we ate had to be boiled or peeled. The water that we drank had to be boiled, filtered and refrigerated. Bottled water was not used—I don't think it was available, but soft drinks and fruit drinks were in the stores.

I had a woman from the factory who took my laundry to wash at her home. But I did not like to give Willy's clothes to be washed out of the house. I did that at home. After some wrong starts, finally I found a girl to come for half of the day. In Caracas, the job of babysitters was unknown, so if we wanted to go to a movie or see friends, the maid slept in our house, which was not too frequent. Live-in household help was available, but it was expensive. Many people like us had only maids for half a day, especially people who did not have children.

For New Year's Eve weekend of 1951-52, we decided to drive to old Maracay, to see what was going on at the hotel. We also hoped to visit some old acquaintances if they were still living there. One couple

Edith, Willy and Karl Mautner, 1951

was still there and we had a big welcome from them, as well as from our old waiter. On the afternoon of January 1st, as we started to drive home, a drunken driver hit us. Luckily it was just the car that was damaged, but we were unable to drive home. As Karl had to be in the office the next day and the repair would take a few days, we had to leave the car in a garage with a mechanic. The mechanic assured us that the car would be fixed by the end of the week and that Karl would be able to return then to pick up the car. At that time cars were made of heavier metal (ours was a 1948 Chevrolet) and were relatively easy to repair. In Venezuela, there were a lot of fender benders, as people did not obey the traffic rules too much, creating a big business for auto repairmen. In general, people drove more slowly than here in the United States, so most accidents were minor. We had our car insurance with no deductible, which when I later started to drive was very helpful to me. I had to use it frequently, because the entrance to my garage was very narrow.

In Spring of 1952, when Karl was about one year on the job, he had vacation time and we decided to drive to the little fishing village of Higuerote. Whenever possible Karl liked to leave the city for a change of scenery or just to relax. He also liked hiking very much, but in the tropical climate of Venezuela this was not feasible. At the time when we drove to Higuerote

Karl Mautner, 1952

there was no road connection from Macuto, the actual beach resort for Caraquenos. It was a long and very hot drive (our car did not have air conditioning) to our destination. On the way were big cacao plantations. Actually they say the best chocolate grows in Venezuela. We stopped and saw those fruits on the trees and decided to pick one and take it home. As Karl was always very fond of chocolate, we thought we would harvest it ourselves and enjoy it. When we opened the fruit, which looked like a big yam with a hard skin, there was definitely no chocolate to eat. It was a greasy brown stuff with a kernel inside, which we tried to dry. We thought that when it was dry, we could grind it and use it like cacao, but it became smelly and we had to throw it out—so no homemade fresh chocolate.

In the village was a small hotel. The owners were Europeans and the food was very tasty. There was only one drawback, however. All the food they served had to be brought from Caracas, and was not delivered daily, so there wasn't much variety. They served excellent fresh fish, though. In the morning fishermen came with fresh oysters, which you bought straight from the boat, broke open and ate them. We tried and did not like them and up to this day, I am not very fond of raw oysters.

The village had a nice beach with white sand and very shallow and calm water, with very small waves. We all enjoyed it very much. One day we decided to rent a boat. As there was no pier, we had to wade through the water to the boat and then climb in. It was no big adventure to get into the boat, since the water was so shallow. The boatman took us up a river, where according to him, big crocodiles lived. We did not see any; he told us we would have to come early in the morning or late afternoon so see them. As I was not too crazy to make the acquaintance of a big crocodile or alligator, I did not miss it, but I enjoyed the boat ride through the jungle. It was picture perfect.

During February in 1952, Willy turned four years old and that was time in Venezuela to enroll a child in pre-kindergarten. In Venezuela, for a child to enter first grade he had to have a little knowledge of reading (being able to read and write his own name) and being able to count and add up to ten. It was important for the child to go to a good pre-school or kindergarten. The school year started in September. Public school was out of question. There was a Jewish school, which had actually a good reputation, but we did not feel Willy should learn Hebrew as a second language right away and Yiddish in higher grades. Naturally there were some Catholic schools, besides other private schools. We did not believe in religious schools as in life you have to be comfortable with different people and not feel superior or inferior because of your religion.

We enrolled Willy in a private school where no religion was taught. The school was in a very good neighborhood, so we assumed he would have nice schoolmates. We had a few boys in Willy's age living in our street block and every boy was enrolled in a different school, so in the morning there was quite a bit of traffic with those big school buses picking up the children.

A FATEFUL DAY

We celebrated the last day of Chanukah on Friday, the 19th of December. We had a couple from Karl's office for dinner and gave Willy his Chanukah presents. As we lived in an area where there were no Jewish children, we always divided his presents; he received something for Chanukah and something for Christmas. We wanted to avoid an event that happened to another couple. They gave their boy a present every day of Chanukah. That year Chanukah was in early December. At Christmas time, the boy decided he did not want to be Jewish because he wanted some presents for Christmas like the other children in the neighborhood. In Venezuela as in America, it was customary to put presents for the children under the tree during the night, so that when they woke they would see their presents. Sometimes from six o'clock in the morning, you heard children in the street laughing and showing off their presents to each other and we did not want to deprive Willy of this pleasure.

That December we were having trouble with household help, so we decided to get a washing machine so that I could wash our clothes myself. Some people told us that when leaving Venezuela American personnel sold their household goods and that we might buy a used one from them. We saw an advertisement in the paper for a used washing machine on the coast. As we liked to go on Sundays to the beach, we decided we would look at it. On the way down we had our doubts, because being close to the ocean, the salty air might have damaged the motor, but we looked at the machine anyway. Though we did not buy it, we bought a table lamp and drove to a beach, where usually we did not go. It was a sandy beach adjacent to a club. As it was close to lunchtime, Karl decided he would go for a swim, while I stayed with Willy, and then we would have lunch. We never went together to swim, as we did not want to leave Willy alone on the beach, as he might want to follow us.

When Karl was in the water for a little while, I waved to him to come out so that we could have lunch. I found it very strange that he did not wave back. At first I thought he did not see me, but as he did not respond I got alarmed after a while and frankly did not know what to do. By that time other people on the beach who realized that I did not get any answer swam toward him and brought Karl back. I believe by that time he was unconscious, because someone called for an ambulance. Completely strange people promised that they would take care of Willy, so that I could go with my husband to the hospital. In the hospital he was put into an iron lung to revive him, but it was useless and he was pronounced dead. The last I saw of Karl was only his face, as his head alone was visible to me, while his body was encased in the iron lung.

At the same time I was given the news about Karl, I was approached by news reporters to give them more information. They took photos of me, which were published the next day in different Caracas newspapers. At that moment I did not know what to say, I just wanted to get back to my child and get home. To say the least, I did not enjoy my fifteen minutes of fame.

At the hospital I was told that I should call a

relative when I returned home, but of course I did not have relatives in Caracas. They then suggested that I call my husband's boss, but he was on a skiing trip in Canada. Finally I asked to connect to the manager of the office, Mr. Scharf. The ambulance driver offered to take me to the car and drive me home. When I finally saw Willy, he was very happy to see me and told me that some people had bought him an ice cone that was made with shaved ice with some fruit juice—he always wanted it, but we did not buy it because we were not sure with what kind of water the ice was made.

When Willy asked me where his daddy was, I told him he was in heaven and at the next question I told him that he would return. This was one of the biggest mistakes I ever made in my life. You should never lie to a child. Many years later he told me, "How I can trust you when you lied once to me?" When Willy was already in college and we spoke about it, he realized that at that time I was unable to answer his question, as I, myself, could not understand what happened.

When we came to the car, it was naturally locked and Karl had the key. Luckily, we had a second set of keys with the house keys in the car. The driver broke the small side window of the car, where we found the keys and started to drive home. When we arrived home, I wanted to pay him—not only had he driven me home, he still had to find some transportation to get home by himself. Here I found out how good people are—he did not accept any payment.

When we arrived at our house, Mr. and Mrs. Scharf, the office manager, and Mr. and Mrs. Klein, were already there. Our old friends the Grunspans and many of our neighbors were in front of the house. It must have taken us more than two hours to arrive home. How Mr. Scharf notified everybody, I never asked or found out, but I don't believe the other people had phones, so he must have driven to everybody with the news. I don't remember that I had met Mrs. Scharf or Mrs. Klein before, but later we became good friends. Mrs. Klein became one of my best friends and advisors that I had in Caracas. She was a survivor of Auschwitz and had many physical problems, which were a result of her time in the concentration camp. Later when I was living in California, they went yearly for medical treatments to the Mayo Clinic in Rochester, Minnesota, and spent then some time in Los Angeles where they had some old friends. I always tried to meet them there and spend a weekend with them. Mr. Klein lived in Shanghai during the war years. I always referred to those people as Mr. or Mrs., as they were older than me and according to German custom I addressed them that way or the German "Sie." I was mostly addressed as Edith, although later when some of them became close friends of mine, I addressed them by their first name.

When I returned home, Mr. Scharf told me that he and the office where Karl worked would take care of the funeral and whatever had to be taken care of. As it involved the moving of the body from one city to another, the casket had to be sealed. Although it was my wish I was not able to see Karl again.

The different ladies present were practical and told me that for the funeral I would have to have to wear black clothing, a South American custom. At that time I did not worry about clothing, as I mentioned to them, I am not going to a fashion show and besides I did not have a black dress. I hated black clothing and still do. So Mrs. Klein, who at that time was about my size, brought me a suit, shoes and a handbag the next day. I had a white blouse and that was allowed.

The first night Mr. Scharf stayed with me, and the next two nights I was also not left alone, but then I decided I had better get used to it and not depend on people. The funeral was on Tuesday afternoon. As it was just before Christmas, the traffic was horrible as it is always during that time of the year. Some people were not able to reach the cemetery in time. Willy stayed with neighbors, with whose children he always played. I believed, and still believe, that small children don't belong at funerals. Besides, I would have had to explain to him the reason why we were at the cemetery.

Mr. Scharf asked me if I wanted to send telegrams to my family. What can you say in a telegram? I said I would write to them. I couldn't call anyone due to the problems with connections. Also, I did not know their phone numbers. I said that after the funeral I needed some time for myself to write those three very difficult letters—to my parents in New York, to my sister in La Paz, Bolivia and to Karl's brother Kurt in Montevideo.

On Christmas day I had a lot of visitors; I believe half of the Austrian refugees came. Some I knew from Los Teques and some from the club we had joined and everybody brought some toys for Willy. In the evening our house looked like a little toy store.

ALONE

Everyone tried to help and console me and not let me be alone. Usually the German and Austrian refugees and the Venezuelans did not socialize very much, especially since a lot of the refugees did not speak Spanish too well. I had no problem in this respect—after all I had a child who spoke only Spanish, although he understood German. All the children who played together on our street spoke Spanish. There was only one little Italian boy in this neighborhood who had to learn Spanish. I tried to converse with his mother in Italian, which was not too successful.

As it was Christmas time, the Venezuelans make a special dish for this holiday consisting of banana leaves filled with all kinds of meat, vegetables and maize flour and then cooked. It takes a few days to prepare it and every neighbor sent some over to me. I definitely was in no mood to eat it. The Scharfs, the Kleins and other friends invited me for lunch, which is the main meal in Caracas. I ate the Venezuelan Christmas specialty in the evening, as I did not feel that I could throw out good food.

My first and very difficult problem was to write to my family. For this, I asked to be left alone for a few hours. Although the letters were sent by airmail, it still took a long time until I got an answer. My mother wrote that she would like to see and help me, but as my parents were not yet American citizens, it would take a while until she could come. To this letter I answered that the trip was expensive and I didn't know what kind of income I would have and that perhaps I might need the money. As much as I would have liked to see my mother, I thought it would be very hard for me to say goodbye to her and be alone again if she had come to be with me.

Lilly wrote that they were planning to move to New York to be with my parents, probably in the middle of the year, and they would pass by Caracas and see if they could help me. By that time, Ernst's brother Kurt and mother lived also in the United States, in Boston. Kurt had left Bolivia about the same time as we did. Ernst was born in Berlin. He moved to Vienna with his family when he was a small boy, and he still retained a little German accent. He did not have to wait for the quota and had no problem getting a visa to the States. He could go with his family any time. However; as I was born in Vienna, for me to immigrate to the United States took much longer. We had registered for our visas during the summer of 1949, but I did not get permission to immigrate to the United States until summer of 1956.

Kurt wrote me that he would help me financially. He even suggested I might think of moving to Montevideo, but he did not believe it would be wise. With my parents living in New York, Willy would have a better future there. My good friend from Vienna, Traude Sterk, was also living in Montevideo. She suggested it would be nice if we could be together again.

For all the sympathy people showed me, I was alone and I had a child to take care of who needed my attention, especially now that he had lost his father. So I really did not have time to mourn. The first morning, when I was left alone, I felt very depressed. I did not see any future for Willy and myself. I even contempla-

ted suicide with Willy, but one thought held me back
—what if one of us survived? When Willy was born, I
made a vow, probably every mother does it, that I
would do my best for my child. At that moment a
neighbor came over to see how I was doing. We talked
for a while and somehow I felt better. Before I never
had much contact with her, as she did not have children. She was much older than me, perhaps a widow or
never married, but somehow she found the right
words to get me over those dark thoughts. In Caracas,
there was no kind of bereavement counseling or
anything similar.

Public transportation in Caracas was not too
good, but taxis were easily available and not too expensive. However, for a European woman, it was not
always safe to take a taxi in the evening. I knew from
the beginning that I had to be independent and not
always depend on people to drive me. As I had a car
and a driver's license, I decided it was very important
that I keep the car and learn to drive. Karl had shown
me how to use the stick shift, but I had driven under
Karl's super-vision only a few blocks.

A couple who worked with Karl in the office
became our friends. They had a son who offered to
take me out several times so that I could practice. My
car insurance had no deductible, so even if the car got
some scratches, it would not cost me anything to have
it fixed again. The driveway to my garage was very
narrow and right in front of the driveway was a big
hole in the street. Although the hole was frequently
fixed, a heavy tropical downpour always washed it out.
My neighbor from across the street offered to park my
car in the garage every evening in such a way that I

could drive straight out. After awhile, I did not want to bother my neighbor. I started to park the car by myself and with this narrow driveway my fenders, especially on the right side suffered. Although my 1948 Chevrolet had a very sturdy metal body, I became a very good customer at the body shop as I frequently had bent fenders. My only inconvenience was that I was one day without a car and the price of only one package of American cigarettes.

Here I have to mention something very funny, as with time I had more practice and my car did not suffer so much anymore. One day I was stuck in traffic, which was not rare in Caracas, and from the opposite direction somebody called to me that he had not seen me for a while and missed me. It was my body shop repairman. This was proof that I had become a good and careful driver.

I had a lot of things to decide and take hold of myself. One thing that I decided right away was that I would never cry or complain to other people, because they would listen to me once and perhaps a second time, but the third time they saw me they would cross the street so as not to hear my problems.

A strange thing happened to me during that time. Willy needed a new pair of shoes. He always wanted ones called saddle shoes, which were half brown and white. Karl found them very unpractical and did not buy them, but there in the store I decided that since I had nobody to ask for their opinion, I would have to make my own decision. If it was wrong, it would be my fault and I could not complain. So, Willy got the shoes he wanted and was happy.

The next and very big problem was how to support myself. Karl did not have any kind of life or accident insurance. Ironically, at the beginning of December, we were talking about how it might be a good idea for Karl to get some kind of accident insurance, as he often traveled to the interior. We did not consider life insurance at all, as my parents had lost money when my father had it and the company declared bankruptcy. We also felt that we were too young to worry about it.

I had learned and worked as a milliner, making hats in La Paz. But when wearing hats became unfashionable and I got married, I quit my job and studied to become a bilingual secretary. I started to work in an office, but the job I had in La Paz was so undemanding that I considered it more as a hobby. After Willy was born, I stopped working and I had forgotten much of my shorthand. I had learned shorthand writing in Vienna in German and had adapted it to English. I taught myself Spanish shorthand from a book, as it was a very good method, but it was so shortened that you had to more or less remember what notes you took. Besides looking for a full time job, I did not know what to do with Willy, as I had no live-in household help.

While Karl was still alive, his salary was not enough that we were able to save anything. We were thinking once Willy was in school, we might be able to start an import business to increase our income. As in Venezuela importing was big business and there were no restrictions with regard to the exchange of dollars, finding the right thing to import would bring us some extra income. As my father was in New York, we thought if he could send us some jewelry that I might be able to sell to some stores. Only much later I found out that I could not compete with the jewelry imported from Italy. When my parents had visited us earlier, my father advised us that his work would not be for the market in Caracas. He was right. I hardly could sell anything my father sent me and when I went to New York, I brought most of the things back to him.

Later, when I was alone, my mother found a company for women's dresses. They sent me catalogues of dresses with samples of material. Whenever I showed those catalogues to people, the people ordered them. They were comparable to the dresses you could buy in the stores, but much cheaper. The dresses were beautiful and also very well made in styles proper for the Caracas climate. I received a commission and on top of it for, a certain amount, also a free dress for myself. That was very nice at the beginning, but the Venezuelan government then raised the import duties and then it was much harder to compete.

PEOPLE CAN BE WONDERFUL

I never expected people to be so nice and helpful. There are too many people to mention. As we had been living only a relatively short time in Caracas and did not know too many people, it amazed me. I was, and still am, very thankful for the way people showed concern for us. Many become close friends to me during the years I lived in Caracas. In the first weeks of my widowhood, people visited me or invited me to their homes. The Kleins, especially Mrs. Klein, with whom I became very close, understood my situation and tried to help whenever possible. On Sundays, they went frequently to Los Teques and always stopped at my house to take us along. Mr. and Mrs. Grunspan also came by and took us to Los Teques, where we went to the Viennese boarding house we knew so well and enjoyed so much. It was especially inviting there with the cooler mountain temperatures.

When I was living in Los Teques, between our stay in Maracay and our move to Caracas, Mrs. Bern and her daughter were staying there too. Willy liked their daughter Lilly very much. Although she was a few years older than Willy, they stayed friends for many years. Mr. and Mrs. Bern were now living in Caracas, not very far from us. They also were checking up on me. I did not have a telephone so they could not call and find out if I was home. When I was home, they picked me up and we went for some ice cream and were invited to their place for dinner.

Often on Sunday mornings, I went to the swim club and got to know the members better, especially the Austrian refugees. There were two couples with whom later I became very close: Fritz and Rosl Popper, and Harry and Thery Gropp. The Poppers came directly from Vienna and the Gropps spent the war years in Shanghai where their daughter Eva was born. Eva was a teenager at that time and treated Willy as her younger brother. Although Austria had a Consulate and Consul in Caracas, Fritz Popper took unofficial responsibility for all Austrian refugees and as I was from Vienna, I belonged to the circle.

Slowly I became a better and more confident driver. One day while the husband of Eva Klein was on a business trip, she suggested to me to go to Los Teques. She was looking forward to some cooler weather. When I hesitated she said to me, "If I survived Auschwitz, I am not afraid of anything anymore. I will go with you. You need somebody to give you courage." She was a wonderful caring person.

Eva Klein was in partnership with an optician in downtown Caracas, and when I was downtown I often stopped by her store, mostly for a pep talk. Eva introduced me to Liesbeth Canfield, who was also from Vienna. She was married to an American who worked for an oil company in Caracas. They had a little girl. Because she was married to an American, she was not part of the Austrian circle, but she had many Viennese friends. At Liesbeth's home I had my first Thanksgiving dinner. Liesbeth lives now in Albuquerque and we are still friends and write or email each other. A few years ago I even went to visit her to talk about old times.

There was one thing that continued to bother me very much. Somehow I had to explain to Willy what death meant and that he would never see his father again. The occasion presented itself when he was playing with a boy from our neighborhood. There was a beautiful sunset, typical of the tropics, and the boy mentioned that God was in heaven and making dinner, to which Willy answered, "Well, my dad is helping him, but he soon will come home." When I heard that, I called Willy into the house and tried to explain to him that there was no homecoming. We both were crying a lot and after a while Willy stated the fact that he wanted to have a father and I should go and look for one. One must understand that Willy was not yet five years old and he loved his father very much and could not understand how to live without him. At that time, if I was sure of anything, it was that I was not going to get married again. After all I had a very happy marriage, where we understood each other very well, had the same likes and dislikes, and tried together to accomplish a pleasant future. I could not imagine marrying again.

Lilly and Ernst wrote me that they had the papers to be able to immigrate to the United States and would come by ship to Caracas, spend some time with me and then fly to New York to live there and to be with my parents. Lilly asked in the letter if they could bring me something. As I knew they were stopping in Curaçao and it was well known that in Curaçao the cost of any perfume was much cheaper than in Venezuela, I asked them to buy me some. When they arrived they had not bought any for me, because Lilly said it was not cheaper than what they sold in Bolivia in their store. However, she was not familiar with the prices in Venezuela.

Willy was very happy to meet his cousin Freddie and the two boys got along wonderfully. When Freddie arrived, he was very skinny and looked kind of sick. According to Lilly, he did not like the food on the ship and did not eat. The ship they arrived on was not like today's cruise ships and they did not have the best cabin. The only thing I can say is that whatever I served the child, he enjoyed eating. That was also the case later when Freddie came to California to spend the summer vacations with us. I was also shocked, when I opened a bottle of beer for Ernst, that they tried to serve some to Freddie. As Lilly said, "The Bolivians give their kids beer and they grow up healthy." In my house he did not get any beer, and I think my objecttion impressed Lilly so much that this was the end of Freddie's beer drinking until he was grown.

Although Lilly and Ernst had written to me that they would help me and advise me how I could support myself, when they arrived in Caracas they treated it more like a vacation. By that time, I felt secure with my driving and driving around was something they enjoyed very much. I did not mind, as I was happy to be with my family and Willy was especially happy to be with his cousin. Besides, if anything was cheap in Venezuela, it was gasoline.

Willy, age 5

A VERY DIFFICULT 1953

After Lilly and Ernst left, it was time to look for a school for Willy. I was not impressed with the pre-kindergarten school he went to. I never had any contact with the parents of the children, or the children, because this school never had any school functions to see what they were really doing. The children were usually picked up by school buses in the morning and returned in the afternoon. For this reason, there was no way to familiarize myself with the school population.

I finally found one that I really liked. The owner or principal was a refugee from Czechoslovakia. The name of the school was "Escuela de Musica de Emil Friedman" (School of Music by Emil Friedman.) There was not very much musical instruction, because for musical lessons you had to pay extra, which I definitely could not afford. Sometimes Mr. Friedman played some violin and showed the children different instruments. The student body was mixed, with European and Venezuelan children of different faiths. I knew the parents of two little boys who would be with Willy in the same class and I liked this idea. There was a woman from Israel to teach the Jewish children, and a Catholic priest for the Catholic children. In Venezuela there were few people of Protestant or Lutheran faith or any other religion. Willy's teacher in kindergarten was from Austria, a very pleasant person, whom I met sometimes in private.

By that time I also realized that with the import business, I would not be able to support myself. I tried

INSTITUTO CERVANTES

INSCRITO EN EL M. E.
PRIMARIA · SECUNDARIA
—
AV. CALIFORNIA · URB. LAS MERCEDES
CARACAS · VENEZUELA

AÑO _____ GRADO _____

Nombre y apellido: *Willy Mauhner*
Fecha y lugar de nacimiento:
Fecha ingreso: Plantel procedencia:
Fecha egreso: Causa:
Dirección:
El suscrito, declara su conformidad con las disposiciones contenidas en el Reglamento del Instituto.

FIRMA DEL REPRESENTANTE

Willy's First Grade Certificate

also some importing from Israel, but that is another story. In Venezuela, bilingual secretaries were well paid and this way I believed I would have enough of an income to support both of us. At that time there were no Dictaphones, at least not in Caracas; so if you wanted to work as a secretary, it was very important that you knew shorthand. My German shorthand was still perfect and to transfer it to English was not too difficult for me. But with the Spanish shorthand I used in Bolivia, I was not comfortable, as it was too abbreviated and you had to remember what was dictated to you. In the evenings after Willy was in bed, I reviewed my shorthand, which was not an easy task.

One reason why I tried to do something with importing was that I had no one to take care of Willy. Finally, I had an honest maid, but she only was able to come to my house for half a day, as she had small children. She was such a good girl. I tried to explain to her that you don't have to have a baby every year. I believe she was not married, but I was not successful in teaching her about birth control. So I had to look for a girl who slept in my house, hoping that I would be satisfied with her.

Toward the end of the year, Mr. Gropp told me that in the office of Metro Goldwyn Mayer, the movie company where he was an accountant, the secretary to the manager was resigning. We both found out later that she was being dishonest. She wanted a raise in her salary and as she did not get it, she resigned and wanted to prove that she couldn't be replaced. This was especially underhanded, since she was also a refugee from Germany. There was an unspoken code among Jewish refugees to support and trust each other. We were especially offended that she broke that code. I came in very unsure about my competence, and to make matters worse Mr. Gropp went on vacation the day I started to work and was unable to help me. When it rains it pours. Two days before I was supposed to start to work, Willy came down with chicken pox. One pox was in his ear and he cried the whole night because of the pain. So I was not in good shape to start a new job. I don't need to mention that I did not last very long.

I tried to import some merchandise from Israel and wrote them I would be interested to have some samples of dresses, proper for the climate of Caracas, Venezuela. I assumed that I would get some catalogues with some samples of materials like those I received from the United States. They sent me over a dozen dresses, which were completely unsuitable for the tropical climate of Caracas and I had to pay duty for them, which was not cheap. I had to pay for the dresses, too. The dresses were very nice and of good quality, but nobody wore wool dresses in Caracas. Apparently in Israel, they did not realize that Venezuela was a tropical country. The contact I had in Israel was a person who lived for a while in La Paz and did not realize that the altitude and climate in Caracas was different from La Paz. The only wool I ever wore in Caracas was during morning or evening hours were light wool cardigans. I was never able to sell those dresses or get new orders for them. Many years later when I arrived in New York, I donated the dresses to a Jewish organization that sent them back to a charity in Israel. I am sure the organization receiving those dresses wondered about getting a whole collection of new beautiful merchandise.

All this happened around the first anniversary of Karl's death. I believe that was the most difficult time I ever had in my life. Everything went wrong and I can only say that because of being by nature an optimist and with the help of other people, I was able to overcome all those setbacks and somehow continue to fight. So 1953 came to an end.

NEW YEAR, NEW HOPE

The store that Eva Klein had was in a down-town office building. One day she was approached by a German importer, who had an office in the same building, who asked if she knew of somebody who could work for him for a few weeks as a secretary who knew English, German and Spanish. She recommend-ed me and I started to work there. Not only was he very satisfied with my work, but he also gave me the confidence that I would be able to work as a bilingual secretary.

By the time I finished this job, Liesbeth Can-field told me that a friend of hers, Franz Richetti[10], who was an accountant for Universal Pictures, was looking for a secretary, as the one they had got a better paying job and wanted to leave. She promised that she would instruct whoever would follow her, which is what she really did. She even came an extra morning to the office to show me the different things I had to take care of. I hoped that this was the proper job for me. Franz also said he would help me. I got the job and did not have any problems with my boss, who was from Cuba. He was satisfied with the work I did.

---

[10] Here I just want to mention how small the world is. I married Julius in San Francisco on November 4, 1956. Instead of sending wedding announcements to my friends to Caracas, we decided to send New Year's cards. When I showed Julius my address book and he saw the name Richetti, he told me that he knew him from Vienna, as they had worked together at the Shell Oil Company.

226

Once when the manager from MGM came to the office he looked very surprised to see me.

At that time when you needed copies of a letter, you had to include in the typewriter pages for the number of copies you needed and each sheet was separated with a carbon paper. The problem with this method was if you made a typing error, you had to erase the error on each sheet separately. The office in New York requested copies for the different departments in different colors and those letters went out by airmail. Airmail was not always trusted, so one copy went by regular mail and I also had to have a copy for my file. Now with computers things are much easier.

The job at Universal also had a big advantage for me because I started to work early in the morning and left relatively early in the afternoon, so I was able to come home, help Willy with homework and be with him. In Caracas, children had homework beginning in kindergarten.

To improve my English, which was not too good, I tried to read as much as possible in English and Mr. Gropp, who got the newest books through the Book-of-the-Month Club, was a big help. I was not even familiar with the names of different authors, as most of my reading material used to be in German. Going to English-speaking movies also helped.

Around the time I started working for Universal, Liesbeth's husband was transferred to Colombia. She had an Italian couple working for her and she recommended that I should hire them. The wife did the housework and the husband had another job. As I was able to provide housing for them, I was able to pay her less, so it was a good situation for us all.

Liesbeth was very satisfied with them. As I was not too happy with the girl I had, I hired this couple. I felt very sorry that Liesbeth was leaving, as I lost a very good friend. Since most people I knew were much older than I, Liesbeth was an especially close friend. She was my own age and she had even lived in Vienna very close to where I had lived. Because of our common background we were able to communicate very well.

As Liesbeth and her husband planned to retire in California, and the Kleins also planned to move there one day, we all often joked about how I might someday get there too. In the end I was the first to settle in California. Liesbeth moved later to Los Angeles, but now is living in Albuquerque. The Kleins vacationed in Los Angeles and I was able to see them when they visited.

While Karl was still alive, I often had trouble with my appendix. We were thinking it might be a good idea for me to go to New York for the surgery to remove it and visit my family at the same time, not realizing that the treatment of acute appendicitis should not be postponed. On a Saturday morning, a few weeks after I had been working at Universal Pictures, I had a very painful appendicitis attack. I knew I could not postpone it any longer. I called my physician, who was also from Vienna. By that time he and his wife were also personal friends of mine. He recommended a surgeon. I called Mr. Klein who took me to the hospital and Mrs. Klein took care of Willy and later she came to the hospital. It was the right thing to do as the appendix was by that time infected. I was told the whole surgery took about twenty minutes. My scar was very small, about one-and-a-half inches and the incision was held together with only one stitch. But there was another problem. Because my surgeon was opposed to giving any pain-killing medication before the effect of the anesthetic wore off, it was very painful when I woke up. It was Mrs. Klein who stayed with me the whole time holding my hand and I will never forget that. Years later when I visited the Kleins in Los Angeles, we talked about my surgery and how she stood by and tried to help me as much as possible. In the hospital Eva Klein also assured me that from now on everything would be better and that the worst in every aspect was over.

The next day somebody brought Willy to the hospital, so that he would not worry about me. Thankfully, I had this couple working for me while I was in the hospital and I knew Willy was well taken care of. I was able to go home after five days and after nine days I was back on the job. Although Willy saw me in the hospital, I believe there was something that must have bothered him very much, because one day he asked me what would happen to him if I would die like his dad. I tried to assure him that this would not happen to me, but on the other hand I assured him he would not be lost—friends whom he liked very much like the Gropp family would take care of him temporarily and later he would either move to be with my parents in New York or to Uncle Kurt in Montevideo. It was a very difficult discussion to have with a six-year-old boy.

After the surgery my life started to get more normal. I was able to manage the job and liked it, had very nice co-workers and at the beginning Franz

Richetti really helped me whenever I had any kind of problem. One of my co-workers often complimented me on the dresses I wore. When she found out that I had my dresses imported from the States, she asked me if I could also get some for her and her sisters. By that time, the import duties for clothing were very high, so I told her because of the import duties it was not worthwhile to bring clothing from the United States. She informed me that she had a good friend who was a pilot for the Venezuelan Airline and that he would be able to take the boxes in the cockpit without any problem. This way I still got my American dresses and she and her sisters were happy too, as we didn't have to pay any duty. Unfortunately, I was not able to import dresses for anyone else anymore.

SUMMER OF 1954

In the Spring of 1954, my mother suggested that I send Willy to New York for the summer, where he could join Freddie at summer camp for several weeks. As I was working and Willy would be alone with just the maid, I liked the idea. Willy also liked the idea, as he was fond of Freddie. As I knew many people who traveled regularly from Caracas to New York, I started to look around for somebody who would take care of Willy during the trip. The wife of Karl's former boss was planning to go to New York during May and she gladly promised me to watch Willy, although he told us he was a big boy—after all he was six years old and did not need supervision. He left during May and my parents wrote me that he was very happy to be there. But during August, he came down with the measles (Willy always got the childhood diseases at the worst time) and then he became home-sick. Although I had already made arrangements for somebody to travel with Willy home so that he would not travel alone, my parents did not feel like waiting and as soon as he was able to travel they sent him home. He was very glad to be back in Caracas and later told me on the return flight he was very scared. The flight was a bumpy flight and he was sitting in the last row seated together with a stewardess.

The timing of Willy's trip worked very well out for me, as the Italian couple I had working for me wanted to leave because the husband got a better paying job somewhere in the interior of Venezuela. After they left I found out they were not too honest, so it was good that they left. I found my old cleaning girl and she was happy to come again. She cleaned the house and did the laundry. For lunch I went to a little restaurant close to the office, which served European food. I had mostly sandwiches for dinner. Very often I was invited out in the evenings. In Caracas my main meal was lunch.

I always enjoyed playing tennis, but I needed a partner. The people I knew who played tennis at the club had their own group and did not invite me to play with them. I was probably not as good a player as they were anyway. I found out that Thea Grunspan's sister-in-law, Vera, liked to play tennis and did not have a partner either. So on Wednesdays, whenever possible and weather permitting, we got together to play. We were not very good players but were happy when we hit the ball a few times over the net. Most importantly, we enjoyed the play by itself. It was good exercise, because both of us were working in an office. On Wednesday evenings Vera's husband always had a bridge party in their home, so before leaving the house she served his guests some refreshments and then came to the club to play tennis.

Since I did not have to be home in the evenings during the time Willy was in New York, I became closer to Mr. and Mrs. Gropp and her sister and her husband, Mr. Fritz and Rosl Popper. Other couples invited me often to spend the evenings with them. People asked me if I knew how to play cards. Canasta was the game that was played besides bridge. Although I was familiar with playing canasta, I refused those invitations while Willy was home—it was more important for me to spend Sunday afternoons with him, rather than playing cards.

Mr. Gropp and Mr. Popper did not drive. Mr. Gropp had some birth defect on his hand and foot and did not feel secure in driving a car and Mr. Popper was much too nervous and impatient to drive a car on the streets of Caracas. This turned out very well for me, as I had a car and was very happy and comfortable driving. Taxis in general were easily available and not too expensive, but you can't just ask a taxi driver, "I just would like to drive around a little bit to enjoy some scenery or just a drive to the mountains or to the beach." The Gropps enjoyed sightseeing and liked to drive to the beach in the evening to a restaurant for ice cream or fresh coconut. The new highway from Caracas to the beaches, airport and port terminal had been finished recently and was excellent—a pleasure to drive.

The Poppers, on the other hand, went nearly every Saturday night to the movies and after the movie to a pastry shop. Taxis were not always available at those places in the evening. During the time Willy was in New York, I usually picked them up. Sometimes I had dinner with them and then we went together to the movies. Later when Willy was home again, I usually had dinner with Willy and then picked them up to go to the movies. It was one of the few times that I did not put Willy to bed and trusted the girl I had to do it. It was nice for me as well not to go out in the evening alone. Fritz Popper had a big knowledge of classical music and whenever a guest conductor came to Caracas they went and I joined them and he introduced me to classical music. I don't know and could not judge if the orchestra in Caracas was good, but I enjoyed those concerts very much. While I was working for Universal, I also frequently went to the movies during the week alone. Not only did I have free passes to attend the shows, but I was also looking at the movies of other companies to compare how well attended those movies were.

Austria had an embassy in Venezuela. Fritz Popper was not only a good friend of the ambassador, but he also acted sometimes as a representative of Austria. During the summer Willy was in New York, the financial attaché from the Austrian Embassy in Mexico arrived in Caracas to report on different import companies, especially on owners who were originally from Austria. He needed, temporarily, someone to write those reports. Fritz asked me if I was able to do it. Since I had evenings and weekends free and I surely could use some extra money, I agreed to do it. At first, he dictated everything and I was supposed to type it later. But we found out this would take too much time because the financial attaché's stay in Caracas was limited. I was working during the day and didn't have too much time then, but I was able to type as fast as he could dictate, so we found it more efficient to work this way. As the entire report was strictly confidential, it was interesting to me how he rated the different companies, as I knew the owners of most of the companies he wrote about. At that time I believed he overrated some of the companies.

When Willy returned from New York, there was a big change in the office of Universal. The boss who had hired me was let go. There were all kinds of rumors, but it did not concern me personally to find out the reason. The most important thing for me was that the big bosses from New York (the main office of Universal Pictures was in New York, not in Los Angeles) liked me and were satisfied with my work. As replacement for my boss, they hired Mr. Weening. He was originally from Holland and had lived many years in Singapore, working there for another movie company. He was a very pleasant boss, who often told me about life in the Orient and Singapore and showed me art objects he had collected while living there. He was the first person who got me interested in Oriental art and the Orient in general.

Franz Richetti was leaving the company, too, I believe for a better paying job. We decided to give him a farewell party. As the secretary in charge, I was elected to supply everything for it. It was not too hard. We were about sixteen employees, so I ordered eight bottles of Johnny Walker Whiskey, some bottles of ginger ale and Coke, crackers and some spreads. I was mistaken about my supply of whiskey. It was not adequate, so after a little while Franz went out and bought three more bottles. Someone added another three bottles, so in total we had fourteen bottles of whiskey for sixteen people. One of the salesmen, just like myself, did not drink much, so after one drink I mixed Coke with ginger ale, so it looked like whiskey. I knew I had to drive and definitely did not want to be drunk. But the amazing thing at the party was that nobody looked or acted drunk. When later in the year we had our Christmas party, I had learned my lesson and ordered a bigger supply.

So 1954 came to an end. Although it was a difficult year, somehow I managed my life. During the year I became confident, having learned that I was able to support us. I found people who became real friends. Some were much older than I (actually some could have been my parents) and I was able to go to them for advice. To Mr. and Mrs. Gropp I could always go with any problem I had and could talk everything over with them. I often received very good advice whenever I went there with some problem, and believe me there were many. The first thing Mr. Gropp would say was, "Let's have a drink." He liked cognac and I had my sweet vermouth and then we talked. With Mr. and Mrs. Popper, the sister of Mrs. Gropp, it was more social as I went with them together to movies and concerts or other shows. Eva Klein was also very dear to me, as she understood my situation and I was also able to discuss different problems when they occurred.

As time passed and being young, friends and acquaintances suggested I should consider marrying again. Frankly, having had a very happy marriage, I was afraid to get married again, although I realized Willy should have a father and he wanted it, too. Everybody who knew a bachelor tried to introduce me and wanted to be a matchmaker.

As I had a servant living in the house, I was able to go out in the evening after I put Willy to bed. It was safe to drive a car alone in the evening or go to the movies and very seldom did I spend an evening at home, except on Sundays when my maid had her day off. In general the movie houses had well-lit parking spaces, especially in the residential areas where the better movie houses were located. With household help I had often all kinds of trouble and I really depended on them, as I was working and I needed somebody to be home when Willy returned from school. Finally I found an elderly person who was happy to work at my place, as it was easy work since we were only two people. Prior to this, she worked in Venezuelan houses with big families, where it was much more work for her to do. She had some stomach trouble and I let her cook for herself food she liked, like black beans and fried bananas. Sometimes I ate it too; I started to like to eat fried bananas. I also taught her to cook European cuisine for us. She was honest and very dedicated to Willy. She liked to clean up after him. Since I hoped to one day live in the United States, and we would not have a servant there, I wanted Willy to get used to putting his toys away. When I suggested that he should do it by himself her answer always was, "Well, that is my job," and I could not change it. There was another thing I could not impress upon her. I insisted that when Willy returned from school, after he had something to eat, he needed to do his homework. Here we did not agree as she insisted that it was important that he relax his brain and should not study too hard. The maid could neither read nor write, but whatever I told her to do she remembered, like recipes for cooking.

Near the beginning of the year, the employees of the office decided they deserved a raise in their salaries. They had started to form a union. I thought I should get a raise too and my boss agreed. Things turned out a little differently. Although we were negotiating with the company for all the employees, we were considered management according to the New York office, and excluded from the union. So when all the employees received an increase in their salaries, I did not receive one. I thought my boss and I negotiated in good faith and we were entitled to the same percentage of salary increase. As you can imagine I was not very happy with this outcome and started to think that perhaps I should look for another job. My boss did the same and by the middle of the year he got an offer from a French movie company, to be supervisor for all of South America. He kept his apartment in Caracas and whenever he came back, which was about every two months, I did the correspondence for him and had in this way a little extra income.

I was even thinking I should apply for a job with an oil company in the interior of Venezuela, where the jobs were usually well paid, and Willy could have free American schooling. But here Mr. Gropp reminded me how I hated living in Maracay, which was four hours away from Caracas by car. The oil companies were often in the middle of the jungle and could only be reached by plane, not to mention the danger of malaria and other tropical diseases. He convinced me very quickly about the folly of my plan.

During May, Trude, the sister of Fritz Popper came from New York to visit him. She had just gone through a difficult divorce and needed a change. I believe it was her first visit to Venezuela and I, being the official driver for the family, showed her the sights of Caracas and surrounding area. Although she was much older than I, we became good friends. She told me that she enjoyed living in New York and suggested to me that I should inquire at the U.S. Embassy how long I would have to wait until I would be able to immigrate to the United States. The answer was not very encouraging, as the quota for Austrian refugees was small and the waiting list was long. According to the ambassador, I should expect to wait for about four to six years until I would be able to immigrate to the States. This was not a very good report, so I decided to apply for a Venezuelan citizenship. The advantage for me being a Venezuelan citizen was that there was a law in Venezuela that any company could only hire somewhere between twenty-five or thirty percent foreigners. Being a Venezuelan citizen would give me a big advantage for getting a well-paid job as a bilingual secretary.

I applied to become a Venezuelan citizen in 1955. I don't remember if I had to pass a test, similar as required in the United States to become a citizen or if I had just an interview. Anyway, I passed the interview and I was assured that at the next official bulletin, which usually is issued at national holidays, I would officially be a citizen of Venezuela. When I returned to the office after the interview I announced proudly to everyone now I am "a paisano suyo" (your "landsman"). I got kind of a cold shoulder from them, as they told me "you are only naturalized, you can never be a real Venezuelan." This would also have been true even if I had children born in Venezuela—they would also be considered as children of a nationalized citizen. What a difference it was when in 1961 I became an American citizen! My neighbors gave me a party and declared, "You always belonged here and now you are really one of us."

Rosl and Fritz Popper decided to give their sister, Trude, a big farewell party. They usually never had big parties, but this was a special occasion and they wanted Trude to have good memories from Caracas and meet all their friends again. Naturally I was invited, too, as I knew everybody and was part of the group. To my surprise when I arrived at their apartment, there was an unknown man sitting on the couch. Fritz introduced Mr. Julius Foyer to me. He was from San Francisco and an old friend of his from Vienna. After I talked with Fritz and Julius for a while, I found out that he was on a business trip in Caracas. He had an export business in San Francisco and was checking on his new agent. His old agent had passed away and Fritz had taken over the company. They were in correspondence for over two years and as Popper is a very common name, Julius never expected to know this agent personally. When Julius arrived at Fritz's office, they suddenly recognized each other as old friends from Vienna. Fritz asked Julius if he had plans for the evening and Julius replied that he did not know anybody in Caracas and would be spending the evening in the hotel as he was leaving the next day to fly to Maracaibo. Fritz called home asking if Rosl could accommodate another guest, because an old friend from Vienna was in his office. It was in this way that I met Julius, my future husband. We did not exchange any addresses and actually Julius told me later that he had hoped that I would give him a lift to his hotel. This is something I would never have done— after all, this was South America and you did not drive casual acquaintances around at night.

Fritz and other friends often introduced me to different bachelors, but I was never interested. Rosl gave me Julius' address and I decided I might send him a card for Rosh Hashanah. I was thinking of him more as a pen pal, because I wanted to know more about life in California and San Francisco as I was planning to

move to the United States five or six years in the future. By that time my friends Liesbeth and her husband and the Kleins would be living in Los Angeles
and my thinking was that if I did not like living in New
York, then California might be better. I was also cur-
ious about life in California in general, as I was and I
am still interested in life in different places. This is one
reason why later when I had the opportunity I did a lot
of traveling and sightseeing to learn whenever possible
the customs of different countries and people.

When I began my correspondence with Julius, I
did not expect to receive my entrance visa anytime
soon. Our letters became more and more personal and
when we finally met in New York, we were no longer
strangers.

During that summer, Franz Richetti, the former
accountant for Universal Pictures who helped me
when I started to work there, told me that the Gillette
Company was looking for a secretary. I applied for the
job and got hired. I had an increase in my salary, which
I really needed. The office for Gillette was very small
—it consisted of just my boss, two or three salesmen,
an office boy and myself. One of the salesmen was
traveling frequently in the interior and my boss also
traveled occasionally. At those times I was in charge of
the office. The territory of the Caracas office included
also some islands of the Caribbean. One of my duties
was to prepare the bookwork for the accountant. He
came once a month to check the books and prepare
for taxes and to send the report to the home office in
Boston. Frankly, I did not have the slightest idea about
bookkeeping; I hardly knew what debit or credit
meant. As there were more or less the same expenses

every month, Mr. Gropp suggested checking out the previous months' books. After a while I became quite efficient. I never made any mistakes despite never using a calculator, since my boss did not believe in calculators. At that time there were only big calculators, which were sometimes very complicated. The office only had an adding machine. During the years I worked in Venezuela, I never had an electric typewriter, but this was not unusual for that time.

One interesting thing I had to do with the help of my boss was to calculate the demand for razor blades for coming years. This was based on the demand from previous years and taking into consideration the increase of the population and adjusting for future production. It was interesting also to learn that people with dark skin needed less razors, because mostly they had less facial hair. Gillette had hardly any competition and electric razors were not popular, partly because electricity was not available everywhere and electric razors were expensive. For any calculation I used a slide rule, which is now considered antique; but back then, I became pretty efficient with it. It is amazing how with such a simple object you are able to solve often very complicated mathematical problems.

My boss, Mr. Kern, was the only American I met in Venezuela who was completely bilingual in English and Spanish. Now living here in California, it is not something special, but at that time it was, and he was actually from Boston. Here I remember something funny. My boss and I were working on some calculations—he, naturally, in English. I could follow without any difficulties. One day, in walked the accountant and with him together we continued in Spanish. I then went to my office to finish the calculations in German. When my boss heard me, he could not understand how I could calculate in three languages, but at that time it was no problem for me. Today I do everything in English and I depend very much on my little hand-held calculator.

Because one did not trust airmail, once a week I mailed copies of all the mail by regular shipping post. Universal Pictures also did this. The razors for Gillette came by ship, but the blades came by air. This was as a precaution, because the humidity on a long sea voyage might damage the blades. I enjoyed working for Gillette. It was very different from the American companies I knew before, like Sudamtex and Universal Pictures. The way they treated their employees and expected good character of everyone, starting from the office boy, was very impressive.

A BIG SURPRISE

A few weeks before Rosh Hashanah, I mailed a card to Julius' address in San Francisco. As I did not get any answer, I thought he did not recall our meeting or just did not answer casual mail he received. I forgot that I had mailed the card.

Tuesday, October 20 of that year was a national holiday in Venezuela and on that day I became official a Venezuelan citizen. On the following Friday, I received two special pieces of mail. One was from the American Embassy, asking if I was interested in immigrating to the United States as my quota number would shortly be due. I was surprised because I thought I would have no chance to come to the United States for the next five or six years. Because of this, I was looking for a different job and had also applied to become a Venezuelan citizen.

The second letter had a postage stamp from Hong Kong. This was still more surprising, as I did not know anybody in Hong Kong. It was a long letter from Julius, telling me that when my card arrived at his office in San Francisco, he was in Manila; but the card finally reached him in Hong Kong.

All this mail was quite a surprise to me and I was kind of confused about what to do about an answer to the American embassy. Finally I had a good job. Willy was in a school I liked. I had also competent household help. The first thing I did was to see my friends, Mr. and Mrs. Gropp. His first answer was, "Let's have a drink and then let's talk." His first suggestion was that I did not have answer this weekend. My big question was what to write to my parents, who were anxious for me to move to New York. I had begun to have doubts about making the move there. I had friends in Caracas whom I really trusted, but they were, after all, not family. On the other hand, friends are very valuable. Over that weekend, I decided to consult with Mr. and Mrs. Klein too. I always believed and still believe in two opinions. In the end I got the same advice from the Kleins and the Gropps, and I decided to go ahead with moving to New York.

When I told Willy that we might move to New York, he was against it at first. He had spent a summer there and knew more about New York than myself. His reason why he did not want to go was that he did not like subways. They were too noisy. I believe there was also another reason why he did not want to move to New York. He was used to living in a house where he was able to go out to the street and always have children to play. In New York my family lived in apartments.

After much thought, I made my decision, which I believed was the right one. I would move to New York. Since I was a Venezuelan citizen, I could always come back if I didn't like living there. I would stay for one year and during that time I would try to work and this would also improve my English. I would always be able to find a well-paying job in Caracas.

At my visit to the American Embassy, I was informed that within a few months I would be able to immigrate to the United States. When I wrote to my parents about the news they were very happy about it. At that time you needed an American citizen to guarantee that you would not be a burden to the government of the United States. I had a cousin, whom I've mentioned, Dr. Fritz Beckman, who was a physician in New York, who was willing to guarantee for me. He also used to live in Vienna and immigrated to the U.S. shortly before or during World War II.

During this time, I had started to correspond with Julius, never thinking that I would ever meet him. He was living in San Francisco and I would be moving to New York. When at the beginning of the year I mentioned that I might be moving to New York, he wrote back that if I needed some assistance, he would like to help me. I had my parents and my uncle, so I appreciated it, but it was not necessary. It took more than a few months until I received my visa and I got quite impatient until finally I received it at the middle of the year 1956. Finally during July, (nine months after the first notification) the embassy notified me that I would be able to immigrate. Before getting the visa, I had to prove that Willy and I were healthy, which had to be approved by the physician at the American embassy. This was no problem except that at the hospital where Willy and I went for x-rays, they mixed up our names and we had to have made a second set taken.

Prior to having my visa to go to the United States, I did not feel it was wise to make any plans as they had told me it would take years to be able to move and I did not know what other difficulties might arrive. Now that it was secure, I had to make arrangements. As I was not sure that I would be happy living in New York, I made tentative plans that I would always be able to return to Venezuela, that Willy would be able to return to his old school and that I could keep my membership in the club.

I had become so hesitant because people who visited New York always painted very negative pictures about living there. In spite of all the difficulties of living in Caracas, I enjoyed living there. While we were living in Maracay, several American co-workers told us that New York was unique and that life in the rest of the United States was very different. They were right. New York had a lot to offer with regard to museums, theaters and being a very big city. After living for many years in the San Francisco Bay Area, which I enjoy very much, I traveled to many places around the United States, including different mountain ranges, national parks and many different cities. Each and every place is special, with its own beauty and charm.

I had been working for Gillette for one year and was due for a vacation when I received the final confirmation about my visa. My boss, Mr. Kern, not knowing that I had plans to move to the United States, asked me when I want to take my vacation. During that conversation I told him about my plans. About that time, Gillette had acquired Paper Mate and when he found out that I would be leaving the company, Mr. Kern decided as replacement for me to hire two people, one for Spanish and one for English. I was in charge of interviewing prospective employees and I was asked to recommend whomever I found to be competent to replace me. It was quite a challenging experience for me.

Now I had to liquidate my home. Some friends of mine who had lived for a time in the United States, but were again ready to return, told me that I should take along only things like mementos, because household articles I could sell in Caracas for the same price it would cost me to buy new ones in the States. They also advised me to have a garage sale. That was something I had never heard of before. I found this suggestion interesting and I put some ads in the local papers and the following Sunday I had my garage sale. When I started to arrange my things for the sale, I did not realize how much I had and said that whenever I had a household again I would not accumulate so many things. That was one promise I did not keep, if you look at my house today.

I decided not to travel by air to New York, but to go by ship. For one thing, I would be able to take along my belongings without extra expense. I was looking for a vacation, as I really needed some rest, especially not knowing what to expect in New York. One thing I was sure of was that I would not have a vacation for a long time.

Finally I had my household liquidated and Willy and I spent our last days in Caracas in a hotel. Before being able to leave Venezuela, I still had a little problem. The visa to the United States for Willy was on his Bolivian passport, as he was Bolivian citizen, but the Venezuelan Government said as he was a minor and because I was a Venezuelan citizen, he was also Venezuelan. So I had to make a change in my passport and Willy left Venezuela as a Venezuelan citizen, but entered the United States as a Bolivian citizen.

On the way to the ship, my good friends Thery Gropp and Rosl Popper went with us, like little mothers who wanted to be sure that their children were properly taken care of. There was no problem in bringing friends on the ship, so they boarded with us. As it was Erev Rosh Hashanah, they did not stay long.

Being Orthodox Jews they did not feel right in traveling later in the evening. In South America, or at least for me, Reform Judaism was unknown.

The ship remained in port overnight and left very early in the morning. Willy and I were on deck to say goodbye to South America. I left with very mixed feelings. At first, Bolivia gave me refuge and I was very fortunate that I could live there without any fear. Although at the beginning it was difficult for all of us, I will always appreciate that Bolivia accepted my family.

I went to Venezuela with a lot of optimism and hoping it would be a place where we could settle. Unfortunately things did not work out as I had hoped. I lost my good husband there and consequently I had a very difficult time, especially at the beginning. In Caracas, I really grew up and was able to support myself and Willy. I became very self-confident and that is something nobody will ever be able to take away from me. In spite of everything, I enjoyed living in Caracas. While I was there, the living conditions were nice. Although it was in the tropics, because of its elevation, Caracas' weather was quite pleasant. You also felt a certain security there. As everywhere things change— so did the way of living change there too.

During the 1970s I returned for a short visit and met most of my old friends. It was a very pleasant reunion. During 1997, I went on a cruise to the Caribbean with a stop in La Guaira, hoping to meet again some of my acquaintances. At that time, due to the general political situation, I did not consider returning to Caracas for a longer stay. The only friends who were still alive and living in Caracas were Mrs. Klein and Eva Gropp, who was married and had two children and two grandchildren.

The name of the ship we sailed on was the "Santa Maria" from the Grace Shipping Line. It was an early type of cruise ship, quite different from the cruise ships of today. It had a swimming pool, which Willy especially enjoyed, and in the evenings they showed movies and had different kinds of entertainment, but there was no air conditioning. In all the years living in the tropics, especially in the interior of Venezuela, I never suffered from heat rash, but on this ship I got it. For security reasons, whenever we were in any port the portholes were closed and that made the cabins very uncomfortably hot and humid.

Grace Shipping Line poster

As I was not familiar with American menus and cuisine, I did not always know what to order and depended very much on the advice of the waiter. I enjoyed the food very much, especially fresh peaches and salads, which I missed the entire time I lived in South America. I treated the cruise as a real vacation and enjoyed sightseeing whenever we were in a port. Our first port of call was Curaçao. As Curaçao was very close to La Guaira, we arrived there the same day we had left Venezuela. I intended to do some sightseeing, but when I left the ship, I suddenly saw the familiar face of an acquaintance from Bolivia. When you meet somebody like this in a strange place, even if you never had much contact with this person before, you have a feeling like meeting a relative. I don't remember his name, but he told me that he was on a business trip in Curaçao and he had an export company in New York. As it was Rosh Hashanah he did not feel like working and went to the harbor to see what was going on there. He was at the harbor with his agent and they had a car and they offered to show us the highlights of Curaçao. It was a very pleasant afternoon. We then had dinner together and later when I was in New York, he called me and offered me a job in his company. By that time I was getting ready to go to San Francisco, so I told him that I was not able to accept his offer.

Another port where we docked was Cartagena in Colombia. The ship offered sightseeing tours, which I took and behaved like a real tourist by buying souvenirs that I did not need—I still have some. It was customary at that time that that you had a list of all the passengers on your ship, including their hometowns. There were a few passengers who were tourists who made the round-trip journey from New York—others were business people and families who preferred to travel by ship and not by air. Other passengers were

Venezuelans who were taking their children to college, as it was September and time to begin a new semester.

No matter what our origins, all of us were excited to reach New York and to find what the future would hold.

AMERICA

AMERICA, AT LAST

The last few days on the ship were very cool, at least for those of us coming from the tropics. It was an overcast day when we arrived in New York harbor after one week of travel. The weather made the city look very gray, but when I finally saw the skyline of the city up close upon entering the harbor, I was very impressed by the sight. I had seen it many times in movies, but from the ship it looked quite different. I was busy with the immigration officer on the ship when we passed by the Statue of Liberty, so I barely had time to observe it. I know now that it is a symbol for immigrants arriving in New York, but I was not familiar with it then, so it didn't make a big impression on me.

I was finally on American soil. My mother and my sister Lilly were waiting for us and were happy to see us. After so many years of waiting we were all finally reunited again.

On the ride to my parent's apartment, suddenly New York did not look like in the movies. Being used to light-colored buildings, the brownstone houses with their fire escapes looked gloomy to me, especially in the gray light. I admit I felt some disappointment with the city that day. On top of it, the sky was cloudy and this made look everything more gray.

My sister and her family and my parents had adjacent apartments in the same building, which was very convenient for everyone, as my sister and brother in-law both worked and were out during the day. When Freddie, my nephew, came home from school he did not come to an empty apartment. My mother cooked for the entire family. For the time being the plan was that would stay in my parent's apartment and Willy would share a bedroom with Freddie, which made both children very happy.

Willy and Freddie, New York, 1956

My parent's apartment was a block away from Riverside Park. On the second evening, my father took me for a walk to show me the park. We had hardly reached the park when my sister came looking for us. She was very excited, telling us that I had a telephone call from San Francisco and that I should return the call. She was wondering how it was possible that I knew somebody in San Francisco. I explained the whole story, and as I had a photo of Julius, I showed it to her. Lilly looked at the picture and said, "I know this person." Small world! Lilly and Julius went to the same commercial school in Vienna, only Lilly attended the two-year program there and Julius, the four-year program. Somehow through school functions they had met.

On the phone Julius told me that he was going on a business trip via New York to Cuba so we could meet. I was very pleased and looking forward to meeting Julius again after corresponding for such a long time. When I introduced Julius to my family Julius recognized Lilly too. After so many years, apparently neither had changed very much. After being together for a few days and doing some sightseeing, Julius suggested that I should come with him to California. After questioning how, he said we should get married after he returned from Cuba. He said we would buy a car and travel cross-country, as he knew little of the United States and I had not been anywhere in America. This would be a nice way to see the landscape. As a matter of fact, although I have visited many places in the United States, we never made the planned trip across the United States. For me it was also very important that Willy should like Julius. When I told Willy about my plans to marry Julius and that we all would live in California, he gave me a very strange answer for an eight-year-old boy. He said, "The man loves you so he will like me too."

Julius went the next day to the City Hall in New York, to find out what kind of documents we needed to get married. There was a little problem. During the war years, Julius had been living in Manila, during the

the Japanese occupation the Philippines. During the liberation of the city of Manila, all his documents were destroyed by a fire that burned down most of the city. In the City Hall, they informed Julius that he needed a confirmation from the American Embassy in Manila of his loss. After Julius returned from Cuba, he left after a few days for San Francisco. When Julius arrived home, the first thing he did was to go to the City Hall where they told him, "You are alive and we don't need any other proof." So Julius called and said I should come as soon as possible because we could get married in San Francisco without any further documents.

The plan was that I should come alone and as soon as we found a house, Willy should follow. For the time being Willy started school in New York and was not very happy, because he did not speak English, although he found a few Puerto Rican boys with whom he could converse. As Julius said, it did not make any sense to send him to a private school, as it would be just a few months before he would leave for California.

THE FOYER FAMILY EXODUS

Julius and his family also made some detours when leaving Vienna until they arrived in San Francisco. Julius was born on June 29, 1910 in what was Austria at that time, but now belongs to Poland. He and his family moved to Vienna either before or during World War I. In Vienna, Julius went to the Commercial Academy and was trained as an accountant and worked as such until the Nazis occupied Vienna.

His father Moritz Foyer was born in 1887 and died in 1940 in Israel. His mother Regina Foyer–Eigenfeld, was born in 1884 and died in 1977 in California. Julius' brother, Arthur, was born in 1908 and died in 1986. He married Mayorie Garcia, and raised two daughters—Michelle, born in 1952 and Monica born 1956.

Julius' sister, Elfriede ("Ellie"), was born in Vienna in 1916. She left Vienna during 1938 and spent some time in Italy until she received a visa to immigrate to the United States, where she settled in Boston. She married Jack Sobiloff in 1940 in Boston and they had one son, Michael, there. The family later moved to San Francisco, where Ellie and Jack separated. Ellie studied law in San Francisco and worked as a lawyer until her retirement.

Julius' parents had been very active in Zionist organizations in Vienna, and because of this activity were given permission to immigrate legally to what was then Palestine during 1938. His father died there in 1940. During the war, his mother was able to travel by ship via South Africa to Boston where she was reunited with her daughter, Ellie.

Julius and his brother Arthur left Vienna during the fall of 1938 on a ship for Shanghai. After a few months in Shanghai, Arthur found he was able to get a visa to live in the Philippines. After he settled in Manila, he cabled Julius saying that he had a good job waiting for him and that he should join him. Julius went to Manila and discovered that no job was waiting for him after all. The fact was that Arthur had dengue fever at the time and was not aware of sending the cable. Julius ended up staying in Manila. While living in Manila, Arthur learned that the Philippines were a U.S. protecttorate and as such he was able to get a visa and move to the United States. Julius planned to follow as soon as Arthur was settled. During the time Arthur was living in San Francisco, Ellie and her family and their mother moved to San Francisco, too.

Unfortunately, the American-Japanese war broke out and Julius had to spend the war years in Manila. When the Japanese occupied Manila, Julius was interned by the Japanese army. After a few days it was discovered that Julius was an Austrian–German citizen and as such, an alien. He also had a "J" for "Juden" on his passport, indicating that he was Jewish. As Japan and Germany were partners in the war, he was released from the camp after a few days. Still, life during the war years was very difficult. When the American Army finally liberated Manila, Julius weighed less than 100 pounds; his normal weight was 160 pounds. It was also a very dangerous time when the American Army was fighting to liberate Manila and the whole city was in flames.

During the liberation of Manila, the city was burned down and there was a shortage of everything. After reconnecting with this brother, Julius learned that Arthur had started an export business. He asked Arthur to send any merchandise he was able to get to Manila. Due to the extreme shortages, Julius thought he would be able to sell everything. Despite the shortages of merchandise in the United States, the situation in Manila was more dire, so Arthur was able to send Julius merchandise nobody wanted to buy in the United States and Julius was able to sell it. The strangest shipment was a collection of left foot designer shoes. What the people did with only one shoe, Julius never found out, but people were fighting for those shoes. Arthur did not only send merchandise that did not have a market in the United States—he was able to send all kinds of dry goods and also paper products.

In 1950 Julius finally arrived in the United States. The brothers expanded the export business to other countries in the Far East and also to the Caribbean, specializing in paper, paper products and machinery for producing paper. It was during one of those business trips that I met Julius—and it changed both of our lives. Because we had been such ardent pen pals, it felt like we had known each other a long time.

END OF MY MOVING

We were married on November 4, 1956 at Congregation Beth Israel in San Francisco with Julius' family present.

We moved temporarily into a small, furnished apartment and tried as soon as possible to find a house so we could be reunited with Willy. Even with great effort, it takes time to buy a house, especially to find one that you really like and will be comfortable. Finally, during January, we found a house we both liked. We signed the papers and took possession of the house on February 20, 1957, Willy's birthday. We ordered or bought the most necessary furniture and had the things I brought from Venezuela to New York shipped to us and finally Willy was able to join us.

We were very lucky with the selection of the house. It was very comfortable in a one-block street in an especially friendly neighborhood. Our neighbors were more or less our age and had children in Willy's age range. Right away we were included in their social activities, which meant that most mornings we met for coffee. At that time, very few mothers who had children were working. This was the reason we had time to get together. We always had a block party on the 4th of July and often celebrated New Year's together.

At the beginning, Willy had some language problems, because his English was very poor, but with the boys of the neighborhood he had no problem. Somehow the kids found a way to communicate. At first Willy had also a language problem with Julius, as Julius did not speak Spanish and Willy understood but could not speak German, but somehow this hurdle was very soon overcome and we spoke only English at home. Willy did not speak or understand Spanish anymore after that. He wanted to be an American as soon as possible and forget South America.

Willy's Naturalization Certificate

Willy did not lose a grade in school because, as he told me, what he had learned in the second grade in Caracas was taught in the third grade in San Mateo. The only problem he had was with spelling. He had a very nice teacher who tried very hard to help Willy so that he would feel comfortable. She told me that she was going to take some Spanish courses, because she might in the future have another student who spoke Spanish. In 1957 there were not many Latinos in California.

On April 23 1960, I became an American citizen and my neighbors congratulated me and said, "You have always belonged with us and now you are really one of us." That was quite different than what was said to me when I became a Venezuelan citizen. After I became a U.S. citizen, I did not feel like a refugee or immigrant. I was an American and very proud of it.

A CONTENTED LIFE

It did not take me too long to get used to being married again. As in every marriage, there are the ups and downs, but I enjoyed my life and living in California. I met new friends, joined the Reform temple in San Mateo and also joined different Jewish organizations. Although I was never very active in any one, I made new friends and also learned to play contract bridge. As Julius was a very good bridge player, at the beginning people tolerated my playing, but later with practice my playing was not only tolerated, but friends actually enjoyed playing with me.

On May 2, 1962, our son Mark Stephen was born. Willy finally had the sibling he always wished for and we were now a complete family, and we became busy with PTA meetings, Cub Scouts and taking the boys to different activities.

I always liked to play tennis and close to where we were living were different courts where I would have been able to play. However, neither of my boys was interested in learning to play tennis and I could not find anyone who was interested in playing or who had time for it. In Vienna, Julius was an avid tennis player but he refused to play with me—I believe the main reason was when I played with him for the first time I beat him and that injured his pride.

Julius continued his business trips, mainly to the Orient. Later, when Mark was older and Julius reduced his travel time, sometimes I was able to accompany him. In the later years Julius took vacations and we took some very beautiful trips. Once, while traveling in

Europe, we made a stop in Vienna, intending to stay for about one week. However, I had too many bad memories of the period of our departure, so we left the town after three days. It may have been that if I returned another time I would have felt differently, but there are so many beautiful places in the world that I wanted to explore, even in the United States alone. I was able to visit many, this time as a real tourist, which included also visiting many souvenir shops and collecting some beautiful things.

On my first trip to the Orient, I became interested in Asian art and was lucky to find in our area very good instructors for Oriental painting. At first I had some Japanese teachers and later some Chinese teachers. I had a very special Chinese teacher, Mrs. Ting, who suggested I should also study Chinese calligraphy. I was never able to pronounce Chinese, but I found Chinese calligraphy very interesting and with time I was able to read quite a few words. I was never able to read a newspaper—for this you have to be able to recognize about one thousand signs. As this was strictly a hobby of mine, I enjoyed it very much and it helped also my painting, which I continued doing for many years. When I was in China, and also Hong Kong, I was able to bargain in Chinese as I knew how to write numbers and some words, but if you don't practice you easily forget them. Sometimes I feel kind of guilty that I am neglecting it, but since Mrs. Ting passed away, I have nobody to encourage me to continue to study it.

Willy went to college at California Polytechnic University at San Luis Obispo, and graduated with a Bachelor of Architecture degree. After working two years for an architect, he changed careers and worked in construction for many years, becoming chief estimator for his company's Northern California territory. He married Susan Springer in December 1973 and they have two sons, Carl Irving, born December 1982, and Max Richard, born August 1987. Carl graduated from U.C. Berkeley and went on to post graduate work at the University of Texas at Austin, where he completed his Ph.D. in mathematics. He then accepted a Post-Doctoral Fellowship at Harvard University and plans to pursue research and teaching. Max attended Claremont McKenna College in Claremont, California, and also received a degree in mathematics, but with interests in finance and computers. I am a very proud grandmother.

Mark graduated from San Jose State University with a degree in journalism and has made his career in sports writing. He has earned many awards and enjoys his work and the admiration of his colleagues.

After so many troubled years, my life became peaceful and pleasant. My parents visited us occasionally and I went sometimes to New York to see my family. I enjoyed very much being a tourist and after Julius passed away I really started to travel and visited many beautiful places of the world. I have been on the North Pole and the South Pole and many other places in between.

One trip in particular brought back many memories. I returned to Bolivia, more than fifty years after I had left, while on a cruise along the Western coast of South America. The main reason for this trip was that I wanted to see Arica again and La Paz. When I boarded the ship, the trip to La Paz was cancelled due to

266

some unrest in the country, especially in the capital. So instead of my original plan, I made a bus trip inland to a typical Indian village high in the Andes.

To get to this village we crossed the Atascadero Desert and the Lluta Valley. This was something I missed on my original train ride, because we crossed the desert at night. The landscape and formations of those mountains was unbelievable. It looked liked the pictures we had from the moon. The color of those mountains had different shades of gray. I had never seen something like this before. The region is one of the driest in the world.

Lluta Valley

As the people of the village knew that tourists were coming, they received us with music and dancing. As I have many wonderful memories of my life in Bolivia it made me really nostalgic. The women still wore many skirts in different colors and bowler hats. The only difference I noticed was that everybody wore very study leather shoes. A big surprise for me was

West coast of South America, 2003

that when I bargained for some souvenirs the women in the marketplace used calculators. That was very unusual in my time there.

The natives asked me to join their dancing, and to the surprise of the other tourists, I accepted. I had no problem with this dancing, as it was familiar to me. In appreciation, the native people gave me some flowers with which they had decorated their hats. I realized that earlier, when I had bought some of the things they had for sale, that I had tried to bargain in Aymara, the native language as I still knew some numbers. The Bolivians realized that I had some connection to their land and that is why they invited me to dance.

I tried some old-fashioned coca tea there, because I felt a little bit dizzy from the altitude. The tea definitely helped. Arica itself I did not recognize at all, although the big hotel in front of the rock or "El Moro" was still there. As much as I could see of the city itself, it looked to me like a vacation destination for Bolivians. It was wonderful to be back after so

Spinner in Bolivian village, 2003

many years in the land where I had spent so many happy and interesting times.

It is fun to visit so many places and see how people live and learn a little bit about their customs and culture. If only people would try to get along better and not dwell on their differences it would be a much nicer world, because the majority of people want peace, to have enough food and have a decent place to live to raise their children.

All of my travels have provided me with many wonderful memories, but every time I land at the San Francisco Airport I feel like I am truly coming home.

SUMMARY

When I look at my life, I am really amazed at how much happened, both good and tragic. I have never considered myself a Holocaust survivor, but rather a refugee. I was very lucky to have escaped Austria just in time. I was not inclined to despair, although I had moments in my life when it would have been very easy to just give up. It was with luck and my inclination toward optimism that I was able to overcome the difficult times and, ultimately, find enjoyment. That optimism and luck, along with the goodwill of others, played an important role in my life.

On the night of November 10, 1938, when we were forced by the Nazis to leave our apartment, we saw light in the apartment of a neighbor and friend and were able to spend nine days in their apartment until we could return to our own. I can't imagine what would have happened to my mother and myself if we had ended up on the street that night.

Getting a visa to Bolivia was also a life-saving event for us. My father had to leave Vienna at a certain time or be sent to a concentration camp. I also don't want to forget the generosity of the former boss of my sister Lilly. Thanks to him, we were able to spend three worry-free weeks in Italy before boarding our ship to Bolivia. I was never able to thank our benefactor personally.

Upon arrival in La Paz we had big trouble in getting our "Landungsgeld," which had been deposited at the Bolivian Consulate in Geneva. Also, when we finally received the boxes with our household goods, due to a new ordinance by the German government, my father's jewelry-making tools were missing. We were fortunate to find a dental supply store that carried tools that my father was able to use in his work.

Despite the fact that life in Bolivia was very different than in Vienna, I felt very fortunate living there and never missed the comforts I had enjoyed before leaving the only home I had known. I was very happy in Bolivia, although we never considered it as a permanent home, mostly due to the altitude. We always viewed ourselves as immigrants or refugees there.

Initially we lived in one room and shared the bathroom with a dozen other people. It was very different from our apartment in Vienna where I had my own room. After some time we were able to afford some luxuries like playing tennis or going to the movies or taking some vacations. In later years we all had decent apartments with bathrooms.

I met my husband Carlos (Karl) Mautner in La Paz; we were married there in 1945 and welcomed our son Willy Fred Mautner in February 1948. In 1949 we had the opportunity to move to Venezuela. It was not what we expected, but after a while we adjusted to life in Venezuela and enjoyed it.

Then, in December 1952, I lost my beloved husband and had a very difficult time supporting my son Willy and myself. I found out how good people are—although we were only living in Venezuela for a short time, I met people who treated me like close relatives to whom I always could go for advice.

Through strange encounters—it was like a fairytale—I met Julius Foyer, my second husband, and got married again in San Francisco. Finally, when I became an American citizen in 1961, I did not feel like a refugee any longer. I was now a proud American citizen. In May of 1962, my second son Mark Stephen was born.

A successful second marriage ended in September 1997 with Julius' death from a prolonged illness and after forty years of marriage I found myself alone again. But this time it is different. I have two wonderful sons, Willy and Mark, and a very thoughtful daughter-in-law Susan, and two adult grandsons, Carl and Max, so I am not alone.

I have had the privilege to travel widely, both with Julius and solo all over the world and also in the United States. Those trips provide me with many wonderful memories. Once on a trip with Julius and Mark, we included a stop in Vienna. I felt very strange there, influenced by my bad memories. In spite of the many trips I continued to make, I never felt moved to return.

I still enjoy my hobby of painting. Unfortunately I have lost my bridge partners, but still play bridge on the computer.

Despite all of my life's ups and downs, by being optimistic and making the best of my circumstances, particularly my lost school years, I was able to live a happy, contented life. I continue to take pride in my accomplishments and offer this story of my experiences in the hope that others may be inspired to do the same.

ABOUT THE AUTHOR

Edith Mautner Foyer began her life in Vienna, Austria where her father was a fine jeweler and her mother cared for the family. The invasion of Austria by Hitler in 1938 forced the family to flee to South America, where with few resources they rebuilt their life.

While living in La Paz, Bolivia, Edith married Karl Mautner, the father of their son, Willy. After moving to Venezuela to escape the rigors of life in the high altitude of Bolivia, their happy life together came to a tragic end when Karl's death suddenly left Edith a young widow and single parent.

By this time, her parents had resettled in New York. With great resolve, Edith supported herself by working as a bi-lingual secretary and raised her young son in Caracas, Venezuela where she met her future husband, Julius Foyer. Julius and Edith married in San Francisco, California, eventually settling in San Mateo where their son, Mark, was born.

Later in life, Edith discovered the joys of Chinese painting. She apprenticed for many years with a master teacher and continues to paint scenes that she shares as annual holiday cards, much to the delight of her friends and family.

Edith's interest in travel has brought her all over the globe. She now enjoys the fascinating world of virtual travel on the internet as well as attending the symphony and the ballet and caring for her children and grandchildren. This is her first book.

Azalea Art Press
specializes in giving personal attention
to authors who wish to realize
their literary and creative dreams.

To learn more about writing and creating
your next print or e-book, please contact:

AzaleaArtPress.blogspot.com
azaleaartpress@gmail.com

To order more copies of
this memoir by Edith Foyer
please email the publisher
or visit www.lulu.com.